What Jesus Said

A TOPICAL GUIDE
TO THE WORDS
OF CHRIST

STORMIE OMARTIAN

HARVEST HOUSE PUBLISHERS

EUGENE, OREGON

WHAT JESUS SAID
Copyright © 2009 by Stormie Omartian
Published by Harvest House Publishers
Eugene, Oregon 97402
www.harvesthousepublishers.com

ISBN 978-0-7369-2410-8

Printed in the United States of America

09 10 11 12 13 14 15 16 / VP-NI / 10 9 8 7 6 5 4 3 2 1

I love God's Word. All of it. Of course, like most people, I have favorite parts that I want to read more often than others. My most favorite parts of the Bible are where Jesus is speaking. In fact, countless times I have opened my Bible just to read what He had to say. This is not to diminish all the other parts of the Bible in any way, but I have especially found great comfort, peace, and strength in the words of Jesus. For that reason, I have taken everything Jesus said and put it into categories so that if I wanted to see what He had to say about a certain subject—such as forgiveness or love or faith or prayer, for example—I could find out quickly. Every word Jesus spoke that is recorded in the Bible can be found here under specific categories. Not every word He said about a particular subject could be listed, however, for lack of room. And many verses could be listed under several different categories. It was necessary to choose which ones went where and which ones to include only as a reference.

This book is in no way meant to be a substitute for reading the entire Bible. I recommend reading the Bible every day and clear through from beginning to end every year or two. But whenever you want to find out what Jesus said about something, pick up this book and check it out. Hopefully each verse listed here will inspire you to open your Bible to that Scripture and read the surrounding verses to better understand the full meaning of what He was communicating at the time.

Knowing what Jesus said will change your life—each and every time you read His words.

—*Stormie*

ADULTERY

Matthew 5:27-28 ~~ ²⁷"You have heard that it was said, 'Do not commit adultery.' ²⁸But I tell you that anyone who looks at a woman lustfully has already committed adultery with her in his heart."

Matthew 19:9 ~~ ⁹"And I say to you, whoever divorces his wife, except for immorality, and marries another woman commits adultery."

BELIEVING

John 3:10-21 ~~ ¹⁰"You are Israel's teacher... and do you not understand these things? ¹¹I tell you the truth, we speak of what we know, and we testify to what we have seen, but still you people do not accept our testimony. ¹²I have spoken to you of earthly things and you do not believe; how then will you believe if I speak of heavenly things? ¹³No one has ever gone into heaven except the one who came from heaven—the Son of Man. ¹⁴Just as Moses lifted up the snake in the desert, so the Son of Man must be lifted up, ¹⁵that everyone who believes in him may have eternal life.

[16]For God so loved the world that he gave his one and only Son, that whoever believes in him shall not perish but have eternal life. [17]For God did not send his Son into the world to condemn the world, but to save the world through him. [18]Whoever believes in him is not condemned, but whoever does not believe stands condemned already because he has not believed in the name of God's one and only Son. [19]This is the verdict: Light has come into the world, but men loved darkness instead of light because their deeds were evil. [20]Everyone who does evil hates the light, and will not come into the light for fear that his deeds will be exposed. [21]But whoever lives by the truth comes into the light, so that it may be seen plainly that what he has done has been done through God."

John 5:36-47 ◈ [36]"I have testimony weightier than that of John. For the very work that the Father has given me to finish, and which I am doing, testifies that the Father has sent me. [37]And the Father who sent me has himself testified concerning me. You have never heard his voice

nor seen his form, [38] nor does his word dwell
in you, for you do not believe the one he sent.
[39] You diligently study the Scriptures because
you think that by them you possess eternal life.
These are the Scriptures that testify about me,
[40] yet you refuse to come to me to have life. [41] I do
not accept praise from men, [42] but I know you. I
know that you do not have the love of God in
your hearts. [43] I have come in my Father's name,
and you do not accept me; but if someone else
comes in his own name, you will accept him.
[44] How can you believe if you accept praise from
one another, yet make no effort to obtain the
praise that comes from the only God? [45] But do
not think I will accuse you before the Father. Your
accuser is Moses, on whom your hopes are set. [46] If
you believed Moses, you would believe me, for he
wrote about me. [47] But since you do not believe
what he wrote, how are you going to believe what
I say?"

John 20:29 [47] [29] "Because you have seen me,
you have believed; blessed are those who have not
seen and yet have believed."

BLESSING

Matthew 5:3-12 ❧ ³"Blessed are the poor in spirit, for theirs is the kingdom of heaven.

⁴Blessed are those who mourn, for they will be comforted.

⁵Blessed are the meek, for they will inherit the earth.

⁶Blessed are those who hunger and thirst for righteousness, for they will be filled.

⁷Blessed are the merciful, for they will be shown mercy.

⁸Blessed are the pure in heart, for they will see God.

⁹Blessed are the peacemakers, for they will be called sons of God.

¹⁰Blessed are those who are persecuted because of righteousness, for theirs is the kingdom of heaven.

¹¹Blessed are you when people insult you, persecute you and falsely say all kinds of evil against you because of me. ¹²Rejoice and be glad, because great is your reward in heaven, for in the same way they persecuted the prophets who were before you."

See also *Luke 6:20-26; Luke 10:23-24.*

BLINDNESS

John 9:35,37,39,41 ∽ [35]"Do you believe in the Son of Man?...[37]You have now seen him; in fact, he is the one speaking with you...[39]For judgment I have come into this world, so that the blind will see and those who see will become blind...[41]If you were blind, you would not be guilty of sin; but now that you claim you can see, your guilt remains."

See also *Mark 8:26.*

BORN AGAIN

John 3:3,5-8 ∽ [3]"I tell you the truth, no one can see the kingdom of God unless he is born again...[5]I tell you the truth, no one can enter the kingdom of God unless he is born of water and the Spirit. [6]Flesh gives birth to flesh, but the Spirit gives birth to spirit. [7]You should not be surprised at my saying, 'You must be born again.' [8]The wind blows wherever it pleases. You hear its sound, but you cannot tell where it comes from or where it is going. So it is with everyone born of the Spirit."

BREAD OF LIFE

John 6:26-27,29,32-33,35-40 ❧ ²⁶"I tell you the truth, you are looking for me, not because you saw miraculous signs but because you ate the loaves and had your fill. ²⁷Do not work for food that spoils, but for food that endures to eternal life, which the Son of Man will give you. On him God the Father has placed his seal of approval…²⁹The work of God is this: to believe in the one he has sent…³²I tell you the truth, it is not Moses who has given you the bread from heaven, but it is my Father who gives you the true bread from heaven. ³³For the bread of God is he who comes down from heaven and gives life to the world…³⁵I am the bread of life. He who comes to me will never go hungry, and he who believes in me will never be thirsty. ³⁶But as I told you, you have seen me and still you do not believe. ³⁷All that the Father gives me will come to me, and whoever comes to me I will never drive away. ³⁸For I have come down from heaven not to do my will but to do the will of him who sent me. ³⁹And this is the will of him who sent me, that I shall lose none of all that he has given me, but raise them up at the last day. ⁴⁰For my Father's will is that everyone who looks to the Son and believes in him shall have eternal life, and I will raise him up at the last day."

See also *John 6:41-51,53-58,61-65,67,70.*

BUILDING ON THE ROCK

Matthew 7:24-27 ⤜⤜ ²⁴"Therefore everyone who hears these words of mine and puts them into practice is like a wise man who built his house on the rock. ²⁵The rain came down, the streams rose, and the winds blew and beat against that house; yet it did not fall, because it had its foundation on the rock. ²⁶But everyone who hears these words of mine and does not put them into practice is like a foolish man who built his house on sand. ²⁷The rain came down, the streams rose, and the winds blew and beat against that house, and it fell with a great crash."

Luke 6:46-49 ⤜⤜ ⁴⁶"Why do you call me, 'Lord, Lord,' and do not do what I say? ⁴⁷I will show you what he is like who comes to me and hears my words and puts them into practice. ⁴⁸He is like a man building a house, who dug down deep and laid the foundation on rock. When a flood came, the torrent struck that house but could not shake it, because it was well built. ⁴⁹But the one who hears my words and does not put them into practice is like a man who built a house on the ground without a foundation. The moment the torrent struck that house, it collapsed and its destruction was complete."

See also *Matthew 7:21-23*.

CHILDREN

Matthew 18:3-6 ³"I tell you the truth, unless you change and become like little children, you will never enter the kingdom of heaven. ⁴Therefore, whoever humbles himself like this child is the greatest in the kingdom of heaven. ⁵And whoever welcomes a little child like this in my name welcomes me. ⁶But if anyone causes one of these little ones who believe in me to sin, it would be better for him to have a large millstone hung around his neck and to be drowned in the depths of the sea."

Matthew 19:14 [14]"Let the little children come to me, and do not hinder them, for the kingdom of heaven belongs to such as these."

See also *Matthew 18:7-14; Mark 9:37,42; 10:14-15; Luke 9:48; 18:16-17.*

CHURCH

Matthew 16:18-19 [18]"And I tell you that you are Peter, and on this rock I will build my church, and the gates of Hades will not overcome it. [19]I will give you the keys of the kingdom of heaven; whatever you bind on earth will be bound in heaven, and whatever you loose on earth will be loosed in heaven."

COMMUNION

Luke 22:19-20 [19]"This is my body given for you; do this in remembrance of me. [20]This cup is the new covenant in my blood, which is poured out for you."

See also *Matthew 26:26-29; Mark 14:22,24-25; 1 Corinthians 11:24-25.*

DELIVERANCE

Matthew 12:43-45 ⤳ ⁴³"When an evil spirit comes out of a man, it goes through arid places seeking rest and does not find it. ⁴⁴Then it says, 'I will return to the house I left.' When it arrives, it finds the house unoccupied, swept clean and put in order. ⁴⁵Then it goes and takes with it seven other spirits more wicked than itself, and they go in and live there. And the final condition of that man is worse than the first. That is how it will be with this wicked generation."

Luke 11:17-20 ⤳ ¹⁷"Any kingdom divided against itself will be ruined, and a house divided against itself will fall. ¹⁸If Satan is divided against himself, how can his kingdom stand? I say this because you claim that I drive out demons by Beelzebub. ¹⁹Now if I drive out demons by Beelzebub, by whom do your followers drive them out? So then, they will be your judges. ²⁰But if I drive out demons by the finger of God, then the kingdom of God has come to you."

See also *Mark 1:25; 5:8-9; Luke 4:35; 8:30; 11:23-26.*

DIVORCE

Matthew 5:31-32 ⟨⟩ [31]"It has been said, 'Anyone who divorces his wife must give her a certificate of divorce.' [32]But I tell you that anyone who divorces his wife, except for marital unfaithfulness, causes her to become an adulteress, and anyone who marries the divorced woman commits adultery."

Matthew 19:4-6,8-9 ⟨⟩ [4]"Haven't you read… that at the beginning the Creator 'made them male and female,' [5]and said, 'For this reason a man will leave his father and mother and be united to his wife, and the two will become one flesh'? [6]So they are no longer two, but one. Therefore what God has joined together, let man not separate…[8]Moses permitted you to divorce your wives because your hearts were hard. But it was not this way from the beginning. [9]I tell you that anyone who divorces his wife, except for marital unfaithfulness, and marries another woman commits adultery."

See also *Matthew 19:11-12; Mark 10:3,5-9,11-12; Luke 16:17-18.*

ETERNAL LIFE

Matthew 19:28-30 ⟡ 28"I tell you the truth, at the renewal of all things, when the Son of Man sits on his glorious throne, you who have followed me will sit on twelve thrones, judging the twelve tribes of Israel. 29And everyone who has left houses or brothers or sisters or father or mother or children or fields for my sake will receive a hundred times as much and will inherit eternal life. 30But many who are first will be last, and many who are last will be first."

John 4:13-14 ⟡ 13"Everyone who drinks this water will be thirsty again, 14but whoever drinks the water I give him will never thirst. Indeed, the water I give him will become in him a spring of water welling up to eternal life."

John 5:24 ⟡ 24"I tell you the truth, whoever hears my word and believes him who sent me has eternal life and will not be condemned; he has crossed over from death to life."

See also *Mark 10:29-30; Luke 18:29-30; John 3:14-16,29; 5:25-29; 6:27,40; 5:25-28; 10:27-29; 12:24-25; 17:1-3.*

EVANGELISM

Matthew 4:19 ⟶ ¹⁹"Come, follow me…and I will make you fishers of men."

Matthew 9:37-38 ⟶ ³⁷"The harvest is plentiful but the workers are few. ³⁸Ask the Lord of the harvest, therefore, to send out workers into his harvest field."

Matthew 10:5-16 ⟶ ⁵"Do not go among the Gentiles or enter any town of the Samaritans. ⁶Go rather to the lost sheep of Israel. ⁷As you go, preach this message: 'The kingdom of heaven is near.' ⁸Heal the sick, raise the dead, cleanse those who have leprosy, drive out demons. Freely you have received, freely give. ⁹Do not take along any gold or silver or copper in your belts; ¹⁰take no bag for the journey, or extra tunic, or sandals or a staff; for the worker is worth his keep. ¹¹Whatever town or village you enter, search for some worthy person there and stay at his house until you leave. ¹²As you enter the home, give it your greeting. ¹³If the home is deserving, let your peace rest on it; if it is not, let your peace return to you. ¹⁴If anyone will not welcome you or listen to your words, shake the dust off your feet when you leave that home or town. ¹⁵I tell you the truth, it will be more bearable for Sodom and Gomorrah on the day of judgment than for that town. ¹⁶I am sending you out like sheep among wolves. Therefore be as shrewd as snakes and as innocent as doves."

Mark 5:19 ⟨⟩⟩ ¹⁹"Go home to your family and tell them how much the Lord has done for you, and how he has had mercy on you."

John 4:32,34-38 ⟨⟩⟩ ³²"I have food to eat that you know nothing about...³⁴My food...is to do the will of him who sent me and to finish his work. ³⁵Do you not say, 'Four months more and then the harvest'? I tell you, open your eyes and look at the fields! They are ripe for harvest. ³⁶Even now the reaper draws his wages, even now he harvests the crop for eternal life, so that the sower and the reaper may be glad together. ³⁷Thus the saying 'One sows and another reaps' is true. ³⁸I sent you to reap what you have not worked for. Others have done the hard work, and you have reaped the benefits of their labor."

See also *Mark 1:17; 6:10-11; Luke 5:4,10; 8:39.*

FAITH

Matthew 8:26 ⟨⟩ 26"You of little faith, why are you so afraid?"

Matthew 9:29 ⟨⟩ 29"According to your faith will it be done to you."

Matthew 15:28 ⟨⟩ 28"Woman, you have great faith! Your request is granted."

Matthew 17:20-21 ⟨⟩ 20"I tell you the truth, if you have faith as small as a mustard seed, you can say to this mountain, 'Move from here to there' and it will move. Nothing will be impossible for you."

Matthew 21:21-22 ⟨⟩ 21"I tell you the truth, if you have faith and do not doubt, not only can you do what was done to the fig tree, but also you can say to this mountain, 'Go, throw yourself into the sea,' and it will be done. 22If you believe, you will receive whatever you ask for in prayer."

Mark 5:34,36 ⟨⟩ 34"Daughter, your faith has healed you. Go in peace and be freed from your suffering...36Don't be afraid; just believe."

See also *Matthew 8:6,10-13; 9:22,24; 14:27,29,31;*

15:24,26,28; 16:8-11; 17:17; Mark 5:30,39,41;
7:27,29; 9:16,19,21,23,25,29; 10:51-52; 11:22-23;
Luke 4:23-27; 7:9; 8:22,25; 9:41; 12:11-12; 17:6,19;
18:41-42.

FAITHFULNESS

Matthew 24:45-51 ~ ⁴⁵"Who then is the faithful and wise servant, whom the master has put in charge of the servants in his household to give them their food at the proper time? ⁴⁶It will be good for that servant whose master finds him doing so when he returns. ⁴⁷I tell you the truth, he will put him in charge of all his possessions. ⁴⁸But suppose that servant is wicked and says to himself, 'My master is staying away a long time,' ⁴⁹and he then begins to beat his fellow servants and to eat and drink with drunkards. ⁵⁰The master of that servant will come on a day when he does not expect him and at an hour he is not aware of. ⁵¹He will cut him to pieces and assign him a place with the hypocrites, where there will be weeping and gnashing of teeth."

See also *Luke 12:42-48; Revelation 3:7-13.*

FALSE PROPHETS

Matthew 7:15-20 ¹⁵"Watch out for false prophets. They come to you in sheep's clothing, but inwardly they are ferocious wolves. ¹⁶By their fruit you will recognize them. Do people pick grapes from thornbushes, or figs from thistles? ¹⁷Likewise every good tree bears good fruit, but a bad tree bears bad fruit. ¹⁸A good tree cannot bear bad fruit, and a bad tree cannot bear good fruit. ¹⁹Every tree that does not bear good fruit is cut down and thrown into the fire. ²⁰Thus, by their fruit you will recognize them."

FASTING

Matthew 6:16-18 ¹⁶"When you fast, do not look somber as the hypocrites do, for they disfigure their faces to show men they are fasting. I tell you the truth, they have received their reward in full. ¹⁷But when you fast, put oil on your head and wash your face, ¹⁸so that it will not be obvious to men that you are fasting, but only to your Father, who is unseen; and your Father, who sees what is done in secret, will reward you."

Matthew 9:15 ∽ ¹⁵"How can the guests of the bridegroom mourn while he is with them? The time will come when the bridegroom will be taken from them; then they will fast."

See also *Matthew 17:21; Mark 2:19-20; Luke 5:34-35.*

FEAR

Matthew 10:28 ∽ ²⁸"Do not be afraid of those who kill the body but cannot kill the soul. Rather, be afraid of the One who can destoy both soul and body in hell."

Mark 4:40 ∽ ⁴⁰"Why are you so afraid? Do you still have no faith?"

Luke 12:32 ∽ ³²"Do not be afraid, little flock, for your Father has been pleased to give you the kingdom."

See also *Matthew 14:27; 17:7; 28:10; Mark 4:35,39 6:50; Luke 5:10; John 6:20.*

FOLLOWING JESUS

Matthew 10:37-39 ∽ ³⁷"Anyone who loves his father or mother more than me is not worthy of me; anyone who loves his son or daughter more than me is not worthy of me; ³⁸and anyone who does not take his cross and follow me is not worthy of me. ³⁹Whoever finds his life will lose it, and whoever loses his life for my sake will find it."

Matthew 16:24-28 ²⁴"If anyone would come after me, he must deny himself and take up his cross and follow me. ²⁵For whoever wants to save his life will lose it, but whoever loses his life for me will find it. ²⁶What good will it be for a man if he gains the whole world, yet forfeits his soul? Or what can a man give in exchange for his soul? ²⁷For the Son of Man is going to come in his Father's glory with his angels, and then he will reward each person according to what he has done. ²⁸I tell you the truth, some who are standing here will not taste death before they see the Son of Man coming in his kingdom."

Mark 2:14 ¹⁴"Follow me."

See also *Matthew 4:19; 8:20,22; 9:10; 10:32-36; 19:11-12,17-19,21,23-24,26,28-30; Mark 1:17; 8:34-38; 9:39-41; 10:18-19,21,23-25,27,29-31; Luke 5:4,10,27; 9:3-5,23-26,50,58-60,62; 10:2-12,41-42; 13:24-30; 14:26-35; 18:19-20,22,24-25,27,29-30;*

19:5,9-12; 22:35-36; John 1:38-39,42-43,47-48,50-51; 6:26-27,29,32-33,35-51,53-58,61-65,67-70; 7:37-38; 9:35,37,39,41; 10:1-5,7-18,25-30; 12:23-26,44,50; 13:36.

FORGIVENESS

Matthew 5:21-24 ⟨⟩ ²¹"You have heard that it was said to the people long ago, 'Do not murder, and anyone who murders will be subject to judgment.' ²²But I tell you that anyone who is angry with his brother will be subject to judgment. Again, anyone who says to his brother, 'Raca,' is answerable to the Sanhedrin. But anyone who says, 'You fool!' will be in danger of the fire of hell. ²³Therefore, if you are offering your gift at the altar and there remember that your brother has something against you, ²⁴leave your gift there in front of the altar. First go and be reconciled to your brother; then come and offer your gift."

Matthew 6:14-15 ⟨⟩ ¹⁴"For if you forgive men when they sin against you, your heavenly Father will also forgive you. ¹⁵But if you do not forgive men their sins, your Father will not forgive your sins."

Matthew 18:22-35 ⟨ᴗᴗ⟩ ²²"I tell you, not seven
times, but seventy-seven times. ²³Therefore, the
kingdom of heaven is like a king who wanted to
settle accounts with his servants. ²⁴As he began
the settlement, a man who owed him ten thou-
sand talents was brought to him. ²⁵Since he was
not able to pay, the master ordered that he and
his wife and his children and all that he had be
sold to repay the debt. ²⁶The servant fell on his
knees before him. 'Be patient with me,' he begged,
'and I will pay back everything.' ²⁷The servant's
master took pity on him, canceled the debt and
let him go. ²⁸But when that servant went out, he
found one of his fellow servants who owed him
a hundred denarii. He grabbed him and began
to choke him. 'Pay back what you owe me!' he
demanded. ²⁹His fellow servant fell to his knees
and begged him, 'Be patient with me, and I will
pay you back.' ³⁰But he refused. Instead, he went
off and had the man thrown into prison until he
could pay the debt. ³¹When the other servants
saw what had happened, they were greatly distressed and went and told their master everything
that had happened. ³²Then the master called the

servant in. 'You wicked servant,' he said, 'I canceled all that debt of yours because you begged me to. ³³Shouldn't you have had mercy on your fellow servant just as I had on you?' ³⁴In anger his master turned him over to the jailers to be tortured, until he should pay back all he owed. ³⁵This is how my heavenly Father will treat each of you unless you forgive your brother from your heart."

Mark 2:5,8-11 ⁵"Son, your sins are forgiven...⁸ Why are you thinking these things? ⁹Which is easier: to say to the paralytic, 'Your sins are forgiven,' or to say, 'Get up, take your mat and walk'? ¹⁰But that you may know that the Son of Man has authority on earth to forgive sins... ¹¹I tell you, get up, take your mat and go home."

Luke 17:3-4 ³"If your brother sins, rebuke him, and if he repents, forgive him. ⁴If he sins against you seven times in a day, and seven times comes back to you and says, 'I repent,' forgive him."

Luke 23:34 ³⁴"Father, forgive them, for they do not know what they are doing."

See also *Matthew 5:25-26; Luke 5:20,22-24; 7:40-50.*

GIVING

Mark 12:43-44 ⟶ ⁴³"I tell you the truth, this poor widow has put more into the treasury than all the others. ⁴⁴They all gave out of their wealth; but she, out of her poverty, put in everything—all she had to live on."

Luke 6:38 ⟶ ³⁸"Give, and it will be given to you. A good measure, pressed down, shaken together and running over, will be poured into your lap. For with the measure you use, it will be measured to you."

Luke 14:12-14 ⟶ ¹²"When you give a luncheon or dinner, do not invite your friends, your brothers or relatives, or your rich neighbors; if you do, they may invite you back and so you will be repaid. ¹³But when you give a banquet, invite the poor, the crippled, the lame, the blind, ¹⁴and you will be blessed. Although they cannot repay you, you will be repaid at the resurrection of the righteous."

Luke 21:3-4 ⟶ ³"I tell you the truth...this poor widow has put in more than all the others. ⁴All these people gave their gifts out of their wealth; but she out of her poverty put in all she had to live on."

Acts 20:35 ◈◈◈ ³⁵"It is more blessed to give than to receive."

GOD THE FATHER

John 5:17,19-23,29-30 ◈◈◈ ¹⁷"My Father is always at his work to this very day, and I, too, am working...¹⁹I tell you the truth, the Son can do nothing by himself; he can do only what he sees his Father doing, because whatever the Father does the Son also does. ²⁰For the Father loves the Son and shows him all he does. Yes, to your amazement he will show him even greater things than these. ²¹For just as the Father raises the dead and gives them life, even so the Son gives life to whom he is pleased to give it. ²²Moreover, the Father judges no one, but has entrusted all judgment to the Son, ²³that all may honor the Son just as they honor the Father. He who does not honor the Son does not honor the Father, who sent him...²⁹and come out—those who have done good will rise to live, and those who have done evil will rise to be condemned. ³⁰By myself I can do nothing; I judge only as I hear, and my judgment is just, for I seek not to please myself but him who sent me."

John 10:32,34-38 ⟨⟩ ³²"I have shown you many great miracles from the Father. For which of these do you stone me? ³⁴Is it not written in your Law, 'I have said you are gods'? ³⁵If he called them 'gods,' to whom the word of God came—and the Scripture cannot be broken—³⁶what about the one whom the Father set apart as his very own and sent into the world? Why then do you accuse me of blasphemy because I said, 'I am God's Son'? ³⁷Do not believe me unless I do what my Father does. ³⁸But if I do it, even though you do not believe me, believe the miracles, that you may know and understand that the Father is in me, and I in the Father."

John 14:6-7, 9-11 ⟨⟩ ⁶"I am the way and the truth and the life. No one comes to the Father except through me. ⁷If you really knew me, you would know my Father as well. From now on, you do know him and have seen him...⁹Don't you know me, Philip, even after I have been among you such a long time? Anyone who has seen me has seen the Father. How can you say, 'Show us the Father'? ¹⁰Don't you believe that I am in the

Father, and that the Father is in me? The words I say to you are not just my own. Rather, it is the Father, living in me, who is doing his work. [11]Believe me when I say that I am in the Father and the Father is in me; or at least believe on the evidence of the miracles themselves."

See also *Matthew 5:24; John 5:24-28; 8:37-47,49-51,54-56,58; 12:44-50.*

GOD'S WILL

Matthew 12:48-50 [48]"Who is my mother, and who are my brothers? [49]Here are my mother and my brothers. [50]For whoever does the will of my Father in heaven is my brother and sister and mother."

GOOD FRUIT

Matthew 7:16-20 [16]"By their fruit you will recognize them. Do people pick grapes from thornbushes, or figs from thistles? [17]Likewise every good tree bears good fruit, but a bad tree bears bad fruit. [18]A good tree cannot bear bad fruit, and a bad tree cannot bear good fruit. [19]Every tree that does not bear good fruit is cut down and thrown into the fire. [20] Thus, by their fruit you will recognize them."

Luke 6:43-45 [43] "No good tree bears bad fruit, nor does a bad tree bear good fruit. [44] Each tree is recognized by its own fruit. People do not pick figs from thornbushes, or grapes from briers. [45] The good man brings good things out of the good stored up in his heart, and the evil man brings evil things out of the evil stored up in his heart. For out of the overflow of his heart his mouth speaks."

See also *Matthew 12:33-35.*

GOOD SHEPHERD

John 10:11,14 [11] "I am the good shepherd. The good shepherd lays down his life for the sheep... [14] I am the good shepherd; I know my sheep and my sheep know me—"

See also *John 10:1-5,7-10,12-13,15-18,25-30.*

GRACE

2 Corinthians 12:9 [9] "My grace is sufficient for you, for my power is made perfect in weakness."

GREAT COMMISSION

Matthew 28:18-20 ᴖᴧᴖ ¹⁸"All authority in heaven and on earth has been given to me. ¹⁹Therefore go and make disciples of all nations, baptizing them in the name of the Father and of the Son and of the Holy Spirit, ²⁰and teaching them to obey everything I have commanded you. And surely I am with you always, to the very end of the age."

See also *Mark 16:15-18*.

HEALING

Luke 5:13-14 ᴖᴧᴖ ¹³"I am willing [to make you clean]…Be clean! ¹⁴Don't tell anyone, but go, show yourself to the priest and offer the sacrifices that Moses commanded for your cleansing, as a testimony to them."

Luke 8:45-46 ᴖᴧᴖ ⁴⁵"Who touched me? ⁴⁶Someone touched me; I know that power has gone out from me."

Luke 13:12,15-16 ᴖᴧᴖ ¹²"Woman, you are set free from your infirmity…¹⁵You hypocrites! Doesn't each of you on the Sabbath untie his ox or donkey from the stall and lead it out to give it water? ¹⁶Then should not this woman, a daughter of Abraham, whom Satan has kept bound for eighteen long years, be set free on the Sabbath day from what bound her?"

John 4:48,50 ⁴⁸"Unless you people see miraculous signs and wonders...you will never believe...⁵⁰You may go. Your son will live."

John 5:6,8,14 ⁶"Do you want to get well?... ⁸Get up! Pick up your mat and walk...¹⁴See, you are well again. Stop sinning or something worse may happen to you."

See also *Matthew 8:3-4,7,10; 9:2,4-6; 20:32; Mark 1:41,44; 3:3-5; Luke 6:8-10; 7:13-14; 8:48,50,52,54; 14:3,5; 17:14,17-19; 18:41-42; 22:51; John 4:53; 5:11; 9:7.*

HOLY SPIRIT

John 14:15-20,25-26 ¹⁵"If you love me, you will obey what I command. ¹⁶And I will ask the Father, and he will give you another Counselor to be with you forever—¹⁷the Spirit of truth. The world cannot accept him, because it neither sees him nor knows him. But you know him, for he lives with you and will be in you. [18]I will not leave you as orphans; I will come to you. [19]Before long, the world will not see me anymore, but you will see me. Because I live, you also will live. [20]On that day you will realize that I am in my Father, and you are in me, and I am in you... [25]All this I have spoken while still with you. [26]But the Counselor, the Holy Spirit, whom the Father will send in my name, will teach you all things and will remind you of everything I have said to you."

John 15:26-27 [26]"When the Counselor comes, whom I will send to you from the Father, the Spirit of truth who goes out from the Father, he will testify about me. [27]And you also must testify, for you have been with me from the beginning."

Acts 1:4-5,7-8 [4]"Do not leave Jerusalem, but wait for the gift my Father promised, which you have heard me speak about. [5]For John baptized with water, but in a few days you will be baptized with the Holy Spirit...[7]It is not for you to know the times or dates the Father has set by his own authority. [8]But you will receive power when the Holy Spirit comes on you; and you will be my witnesses in Jerusalem, and in all Judea and Samaria, and to the ends of the earth."

See also *Luke 24:49; John 7:37-38; 16:5-15; Acts 11:16.*

HUMILITY

Luke 14:8-11 [8]"When someone invites you to a wedding feast, do not take the place of honor, for a person more distinguished than you may have been invited. [9]If so, the host who invited both of you will come and say to you, 'Give this man your seat.' Then, humiliated, you will have to take the least important place. [10]But when you are invited, take the lowest place, so that when your host comes, he will say to you, 'Friend, move up to a better place.' Then you will be honored in the presence of all your fellow guests. [11]For everyone who exalts himself will be humbled, and he who humbles himself will be exalted."

Luke 22:25-30 [25]"The kings of the Gentiles lord it over them; and those who exercise authority over them call themselves Benefactors. ²⁶But you are not to be like that. Instead, the greatest among you should be like the youngest, and the one who rules like the one who serves. ²⁷For who is greater, the one who is at the table or the one who serves? Is it not the one who is at the table? But I am among you as one who serves. ²⁸You are those who have stood by me in my trials. ²⁹And I confer on you a kingdom, just as my Father conferred one on me, ³⁰so that you may eat and drink at my table in my kingdom and sit on thrones, judging the twelve tribes of Israel."

HYPOCRISY

Matthew 15:3-11,13-14,16-20 ³"And why do you break the command of God for the sake of your tradition? ⁴For God said, 'Honor your father and mother' and 'Anyone who curses his father or mother must be put to death.' ⁵But you say that if a man says to his father or mother, 'Whatever help you might otherwise have received from me is a gift devoted to God,' ⁶he is not to 'honor his father' with it. Thus you nullify the word of God for the sake of your tradition. ⁷You hypocrites! Isaiah was right when he prophesied about you: ⁸'These people honor me with their lips, but their hearts are far from me. ⁹They worship me in vain; their teachings are but rules taught by men.' ¹⁰Listen and understand. ¹¹What goes into a man's mouth does not make him 'unclean,' but what comes out of his mouth, that is what makes him 'unclean'...¹³Every plant that my heavenly Father has not planted will be pulled up by the roots. ¹⁴Leave them; they are blind guides. If a blind man leads a blind man, both will fall into a pit...¹⁶Are you still so dull? ¹⁷Don't you see that whatever enters the mouth goes into the stomach and then out of the body? ¹⁸But the things that come out of the mouth come from the heart, and these make a man 'unclean.' ¹⁹For out of the heart come evil thoughts, murder, adultery, sexual immorality, theft, false testimony, slander. ²⁰These are what make a man 'unclean'; but eating with unwashed hands does not make him 'unclean.'"

Mark 8:15,17-21 ¹⁵"Be careful...Watch out for the yeast of the Pharisees and that of

Herod…[17]Why are you talking about having no bread? Do you still not see or understand? Are your hearts hardened? [18]Do you have eyes but fail to see, and ears but fail to hear? And don't you remember? [19]When I broke the five loaves for the five thousand, how many basketfuls of pieces did you pick up? [20]And when I broke the seven loaves for the four thousand, how many basketfuls of pieces did you pick up? [21]Do you still not understand?"

See also *Matthew 8:11; 16:6,8-11; Mark 7:6-16,18-23; 12:38-40; Luke 7:31-35; 12:1-3; 20:46-47.*

JERUSALEM

Matthew 23:37-39 [37]"O Jerusalem, Jerusalem, you who kill the prophets and stone those sent to you, how often I have longed to gather your children together, as a hen gathers her chicks under her wings, but you were not willing. [38]Look, your house is left to you desolate. [39]For I tell you, you will not see me again until you say, 'Blessed is he who comes in the name of the Lord.'"

Luke 19:42-44 ⟨∾⟩ ⁴²"If you, even you, had only known on this day what would bring you peace— but now it is hidden from your eyes. ⁴³The days will come upon you when your enemies will build an embankment against you and encircle you and hem you in on every side. ⁴⁴They will dash you to the ground, you and the children within your walls. They will not leave one stone on another, because you did not recognize the time of God's coming to you."

See also *Luke 13:34-35*.

JESUS' BAPTISM

Matthew 3:15 ⟨∾⟩ ¹⁵"Let it be so now [Jesus' baptism]; it is proper for us to do this to fulfill all righteousness."

JESUS' IDENTITY

Mark 8:27,29 ⟨∾⟩ ²⁷"Who do people say I am?… ²⁹But what about you?…Who do you say I am?"

See also *Matthew 16:15,17-19; 22:42-45; Mark 8:26; Luke 9:18,20; 20:41-44; John 8:58*.

JESUS IS LORD

Luke 20:41-44 ⁓ ⁴¹"How is it that they say the Christ is the Son of David? ⁴²David himself declares in the Book of Psalms: 'The Lord said to my Lord: "Sit at my right hand ⁴³until I make your enemies a footstool for your feet."' ⁴⁴David calls him 'Lord.' How then can he be his son?"

See also *Matthew 7:21-23; 12:8; 22:42-45; Mark 12:35-37; Luke 6:3-5.*

JESUS' MINISTRY

Mark 1:38 ⁓ ³⁸"Let us go somewhere else—to the nearby villages—so I can preach there also. That is why I have come."

Luke 4:18-19,21,43 ⁓ ¹⁸"The Spirit of the Lord is on me, because he has anointed me to preach good news to the poor. He has sent me to proclaim freedom for the prisoners and recovery of sight for the blind, to release the oppressed, ¹⁹to proclaim the year of the Lord's favor...²¹Today this scripture is fulfilled in your hearing...⁴³I must preach the good news of the kingdom of God to the other towns also, because that is why I was sent."

JESUS' PASSION

Passion Prophecies

Matthew 17:22-23 ⟶ ²²"The Son of Man is going to be betrayed into the hands of men. ²³They will kill him, and on the third day he will be raised to life."

Matthew 26:2,31-32 ⟶ ²"As you know, the Passover is two days away—and the Son of Man will be handed over to be crucified…³¹This very night you will all fall away on account of me, for it is written: 'I will strike the shepherd, and the sheep of the flock will be scattered.' ³²But after I have risen, I will go ahead of you into Galilee."

See also *Matthew 20:18-9; Mark 9:31; 10:33-34; 14:27-28; 22:37-38; Luke 9:22,44; Luke 18:31-33; Luke 24:7; John 12:32; 16:16.*

Jesus' Betrayal

Matthew 26:21,23-24 ⟶ ²¹"I tell you the truth, one of you will betray me…²³The one who has dipped his hand into the bowl with me will betray me. ²⁴The Son of Man will go just as it is written about him. But woe to that man who betrays the

Son of Man! It would be better for him if he had not been born."

See also *Matthew 26:25; Mark 14:18,20-21; Luke 22:21-22; John 13:10,18-21,26-27.*

Gethsemane

Matthew 26:36,38-42,45-46,50,52-54 ‎ ³⁶[To his disciples] "Sit here while I go over there and pray…³⁸My soul is overwhelmed with sorrow to the point of death. Stay here and keep watch with me. ³⁹My Father, if it is possible, may this cup be taken from me. Yet not as I will, but as you will. ⁴⁰Could you men not keep watch with me for one hour? ⁴¹Watch and pray so that you will not fall into temptation. The spirit is willing, but the body is weak. ⁴²My Father, if it is not possible for this cup to be taken away unless I drink it, may your will be done…⁴⁵Are you still sleeping and resting? Look, the hour is near, and the Son of Man is betrayed into the hands of sinners. ⁴⁶Rise, let us go! Here comes my betrayer!…⁵⁰Friend, do what you came for…⁵²Put your sword back in its place…for all who draw the sword will die by the sword. ⁵³Do you think I cannot call on my Father, and he will at once put at my disposal more than twelve legions of angels? [54]But how then would the Scriptures be fulfilled that say it must happen in this way?"

See also *Matthew 26:55-56; Mark 14:32,34,36-38,41-42,48-49; Luke 22:40,42,46,48,51-53; John 18:4-9,11.*

Jesus' Trial

Mark 14:62 [62]"I am [the Christ, the Son of the Blessed One, O high priest, as you have said]…and you will see the Son of Man sitting at the right hand of the Mighty One and coming on the clouds of heaven."

John 18:20-21,23,34,36-37 [20]"I have spoken openly to the world…I always taught in synagogues or at the temple, where all the Jews come together. I said nothing in secret. [21]Why question me? Ask those who heard me. Surely they know what I said…[23]If I said something wrong…testify as to what is wrong. But if I spoke the truth, why did you strike me?…[34]Is that your own idea…or did others talk to you about me?…[36]My kingdom is not of this world. If it were, my servants would fight to prevent my arrest by the Jews. But now my kingdom is from another place. [37]...You are right in saying I am a king. In fact, for this reason I was born, and for this I came into the world, to testify to the truth. Everyone on the side of truth listens to me."

John 19:11 [11]"You would have no power over me if it were not given to you from above. Therefore the one who handed me over to you is guilty of a greater sin."

See also *Matthew 26:64; 27:11; Mark 15:2; Luke 22:67-70; 23:3.*

Peter's Denial

Matthew 26:34 [34]"I tell you the truth... this very night, before the rooster crows, you will disown me three times."

See also *Matthew 26:75; Mark 14:30,72; Luke 22:34,61; John 13:36,38.*

Crucifixion

Matthew 27:46 [46]"*Eloi, Eloi, lama sabachthani?*...My God, my God, why have you forsaken me?"

Luke 23:43 ⬥ ⁴³ [To the thief on the cross] "I tell you the truth, today you will be with me in paradise."

John 19:26-28,30 ⬥ ²⁶"Dear woman, here is your son. ²⁷[Son, here] is your mother. ²⁸I am thirsty...³⁰It is finished."

See also *Mark 15:34; Luke 23:28-31,46.*

Resurrection

Luke 24:17,25-26,36,38-39,41,44,46-48 ⬥ ¹⁷ [To some disciples who don't recognize him at first] "What are you discussing together as you walk along?...²⁵[Reacting to the news of his own death and empty tomb as though he knew nothing about it] How foolish you are, and how slow of heart to believe all that the prophets have spoken! ²⁶Did not the Christ have to suffer these things and then enter his glory?...³⁶Peace be with you...³⁸Why are you troubled, and why do doubts rise in your minds? ³⁹Look at my hands and my feet. It is I myself! Touch me and see; a ghost does not have flesh and bones, as you see I have...⁴¹Do you have anything here to eat?...⁴⁴This is what

I told you while I was still with you: Everything must be fulfilled that is written about me in the Law of Moses, the Prophets and the Psalms...⁴⁶This is what is written: The Christ will suffer and rise from the dead on the third day, ⁴⁷and repentance and forgiveness of sins will be preached in his name to all nations, beginning at Jerusalem. ⁴⁸You are witnesses of these things."

John 20:15-17,21-23,26-27 ⟨⟩ ¹⁵"Woman...why are you crying? Who is it you are looking for? ¹⁶Mary. ¹⁷Do not hold on to me, for I have not yet returned to the Father. Go instead to my brothers and tell them, 'I am returning to my Father and your Father, to my God and your God'...²¹Peace be with you! As the Father has sent me, I am sending you. ²²Receive the Holy Spirit. ²³If you forgive anyone his sins, they are forgiven; if you do not forgive them, they are not forgiven...²⁶Peace be with you! ²⁷Put your finger here; see my hands. Reach out your hand and put it into my side. Stop doubting and believe."

John 21:5-6,10,12,15-19,22 ⟨⟩ ⁵"Friends, haven't you any fish? ⁶ Throw your net on the right side of the boat and you will find some…¹⁰Bring some of the fish you have just caught…¹²Come and have breakfast…¹⁵Simon son of John, do you truly love me more than these? Feed my lambs. ¹⁶Simon son of John, do you truly love me? Take care of my sheep. ¹⁷Simon son of John, do you love me?…Feed my sheep. ¹⁸I tell you the truth, when you were younger you dressed yourself and went where you wanted; but when you are old you will stretch out your hands, and someone else will dress you and lead you where you do not want to go. ¹⁹Follow me!…²²If I want [the disciple whom I love] to remain alive until I return, what is that to you[, Peter]? You must follow me."

See also *Matthew 22:42; Luke 24:19,49; John 20:29; 21:23.*

JESUS PRAYS

Matthew 11:25-26 ²⁵"I praise you, Father, Lord of heaven and earth, because you have hidden these things from the wise and learned, and revealed them to little children. ²⁶Yes, Father, for this was your good pleasure."

John 17:4-8 ⟨≈⟩ ⁴"I have brought you glory on earth by completing the work you gave me to do. ⁵And now, Father, glorify me in your presence with the glory I had with you before the world began. ⁶I have revealed you to those whom you gave me out of the world. They were yours; you gave them to me and they have obeyed your word. ⁷Now they know that everything you have given me comes from you. ⁸For I gave them the words you gave me and they accepted them. They knew with certainty that I came from you, and they believed that you sent me."

See also *Luke 10:21-22; 22:42; John 17:1-3,9-26.*

JESUS PROPHESIES

Matthew 24:2,4-8,34-44 ⟨≈⟩ ²"Do you see all these things? I tell you the truth, not one stone here will be left on another; every one will be thrown down…⁴Watch out that no one deceives you. ⁵For many will come in my name, claiming, 'I am the Christ,' and will deceive many. ⁶You will hear of wars and rumors of wars, but see to it that you are not alarmed. Such things must happen, but the end is still to come. ⁷Nation will rise against nation, and kingdom against kingdom. There will be famines and earthquakes in various places. ⁸All these are the beginning of birth pains…³⁴I tell you the truth, this generation will certainly not pass away until all these things have happened. ³⁵Heaven and earth will pass away, but my words will never pass away. ³⁶No one knows about that day or hour, not even the angels in heaven, nor the Son, but only the Father. ³⁷As it was in the days of Noah, so it will be at the coming of the Son of Man. ³⁸For in the days before the flood, people were eating and drinking, marrying and giving in marriage, up to the day Noah entered the ark; ³⁹and they knew nothing about what would happen until the flood came and took them all away. That is how it will be at the coming of the Son of Man. ⁴⁰Two men will be in the field; one will be taken and the other left. ⁴¹Two women will be grinding with a hand mill; one will be taken and the other left. ⁴²Therefore keep watch, because you do not know on what day your Lord will come. ⁴³But understand this: If the owner of the house had known at what time of night the thief was coming, he would have kept watch and would not have let his house be broken into. ⁴⁴So you also must be ready, because the Son of Man will come at an hour when you do not expect him."

See also *Matthew 5:17-18; 11:21-24; 21:2-3,42-44; 24:9-33; 26:10-13,18,31-32; Mark 11:2-3; 13:2,5-32; 14:6-9,13-15; Luke 12:49-59; 13:32-35; 17:22-37; 19:30-31,42-44; 21:6,8-33; 22:8-12,31-32; 23:28-31; John 2:19; 12:7-8,27-28,30-32,34-36; 13:38; 14:1-4,28-31; 16:1-4,16-22.*

JESUS QUESTIONED

Matthew 21:24-25,27 ⁂ ²⁴"I will also ask you one question. If you answer me, I will tell you by what authority I am doing these things. ²⁵John's baptism—where did it come from? Was it from heaven, or from men?…²⁷Neither will I tell you by what authority I am doing these things."

See also *Matthew 22:18-21; Mark 11:29-30,33; 12:15-17,24-27,29-31,34-37; Luke 20:3-4,8,23-25,34-38; John 7:16-19,21-24,28-29,33-34,36; 8:7,10-12,14-19,21-26,28-29.*

JESUS' RETURN

Revelation 16:15 ⟨⟩ ¹⁵"Behold, I come like a thief! Blessed is he who stays awake and keeps his clothes with him, so that he may not go naked and be shamefully exposed."

Revelation 22:7,12-13,16,20 ⟨⟩ ⁷"Behold, I am coming soon! Blessed is he who keeps the words of the prophecy in this book…¹²Behold, I am coming soon! My reward is with me, and I will give to everyone according to what he has done. ¹³I am the Alpha and the Omega, the First and the Last, the Beginning and the End…¹⁶I, Jesus, have sent my angel to give you this testimony for the churches. I am the Root and the Offspring of David, and the bright Morning Star…²⁰Yes, I am coming soon."

JESUS' TEMPTATION

Matthew 4:4,7,10 ⟨⟩ ⁴"It is written: 'Man does not live on bread alone, but on every word that comes from the mouth of God'…⁷It is also written: 'Do not put the Lord your God to the test'… ¹⁰Away from me, Satan! For it is written: 'Worship the Lord your God, and serve him only.'"

Luke 4:4,8,12 ⟨ ⟩ [4]"It is written: 'Man does not live on bread alone'...[8]It is written: 'Worship the Lord your God and serve him only'...[12]It says: 'Do not put the Lord your God to the test.'"

JESUS, THE VINE

John 15:1-8 ⟨ ⟩ [1]"I am the true vine, and my Father is the gardener. [2]He cuts off every branch in me that bears no fruit, while every branch that does bear fruit he prunes so that it will be even more fruitful. [3]You are already clean because of the word I have spoken to you. [4]Remain in me, and I will remain in you. No branch can bear fruit by itself; it must remain in the vine. Neither can you bear fruit unless you remain in me. [5]I am the vine; you are the branches. If a man remains in me and I in him, he will bear much fruit; apart from me you can do nothing. [6]If anyone does not remain in me, he is like a branch that is thrown away and withers; such branches are picked up, thrown into the fire and burned. [7]If you remain in me and my words remain in you, ask whatever you wish, and it will be given you. [8]This is to my

Father's glory, that you bear much fruit, showing yourselves to be my disciples."

JOHN THE BAPTIST

Matthew 11:4-14 ⟨⟩ ⁴"Go back and report to John what you hear and see: ⁵The blind receive sight, the lame walk, those who have leprosy are cured, the deaf hear, the dead are raised, and the good news is preached to the poor. ⁶Blessed is the man who does not fall away on account of me. ⁷What did you go out into the desert to see? A reed swayed by the wind? ⁸If not, what did you go out to see? A man dressed in fine clothes? No, those who wear fine clothes are in kings' palaces. ⁹Then what did you go out to see? A prophet? Yes, I tell you, and more than a prophet. ¹⁰This is the one about whom it is written: 'I will send my messenger ahead of you, who will prepare your way before you.' ¹¹I tell you the truth: Among those born of women there has not risen anyone greater than John the Baptist; yet he who is least in the kingdom of heaven is greater than he. ¹²From the days of John the Baptist until now, the kingdom of heaven has been forcefully advancing, and forceful men lay hold of it. ¹³For all the Prophets and the Law prophesied until John. ¹⁴And if you are willing to accept it, he is the Elijah who was to come.

See also *Matthew 11:15-19; 17:11-12; Luke 7:22-28,31-35; John 5:33-35.*

JUDGING OTHERS

Matthew 7:1-6 ⌘ ¹"Do not judge, or you too will be judged. ²For in the same way you judge others, you will be judged, and with the measure you use, it will be measured to you. ³Why do you look at the speck of sawdust in your brother's eye and pay no attention to the plank in your own eye? ⁴How can you say to your brother, 'Let me take the speck out of your eye,' when all the time there is a plank in your own eye? ⁵You hypocrite, first take the plank out of your own eye, and then you will see clearly to remove the speck from your brother's eye. ⁶Do not give dogs what is sacred; do not throw your pearls to pigs. If you do, they may trample them under their feet, and then turn and tear you to pieces."

Luke 6:37,39-42 ⌘ ³⁷"Do not judge, and you

will not be judged. Do not condemn, and you will not be condemned. Forgive, and you will be forgiven...³⁹Can a blind man lead a blind man? Will they not both fall into a pit? ⁴⁰A student is not above his teacher, but everyone who is fully trained will be like his teacher. ⁴¹Why do you look at the speck of sawdust in your brother's eye and pay no attention to the plank in your own eye? ⁴²How can you say to your brother, 'Brother, let me take the speck out of your eye,' when you yourself fail to see the plank in your own eye? You hypocrite, first take the plank out of your eye, and then you will see clearly to remove the speck from your brother's eye."

KINGDOM OF GOD

Matthew 13:44-52; 20:21-23 ⁴⁴"The kingdom of heaven is like treasure hidden in a field. When a man found it, he hid it again, and then in his joy went and sold all he had and bought that field. ⁴⁵Again, the kingdom of heaven is like a merchant looking for fine pearls. ⁴⁶When he found one of great value, he went away and sold everything he had and bought it. ⁴⁷Once again, the kingdom of heaven is like a net that was let down into the lake and caught all kinds of fish. [48]When it was full, the fishermen pulled it up on the shore. Then they sat down and collected the good fish in baskets, but threw the bad away. [49]This is how it will be at the end of the age. The angels will come and separate the wicked from the righteous [50]and throw them into the fiery furnace, where there will be weeping and gnashing of teeth. [51]Have you understood all these things? [52]Therefore every teacher of the law who has been instructed about the kingdom of heaven is like the owner of a house who brings out of his storeroom new treasures as well as old...[21]What is it you want? [22]You don't know what you are asking...Can you drink the cup I am going to drink? [23]You will indeed drink from my cup, but to sit at my right or left is not for me to grant. These places belong to those for whom they have been prepared by my Father."

Mark 9:1 ❧ [1]"I tell you the truth, some who are standing here will not taste death before they see the kingdom of God come with power."

Luke 16:15-16; 17:20-21 ✥ ¹⁵"You are the ones who justify yourselves in the eyes of men, but God knows your hearts. What is highly valued among men is detestable in God's sight. ¹⁶The Law and the Prophets were proclaimed until John. Since that time, the good news of the kingdom of God is being preached, and everyone is forcing his way into it…²⁰The kingdom of God does not come with your careful observation, ²¹nor will people say, 'Here it is,' or 'There it is,' because the kingdom of God is within you."

See also *Matthew 4:17; 5:3,10,19-20; 7:21; 8:11; 10:7; 11:11-12; 12:28; 13:11,24,31; 16:19; 18:3-4,23; 19:12,14,23-24; 20:1; 21:31,43; 22:2; 23:13; 25:1; Mark 1:15; 4:11,26,30; 9:47; 10:14-15,23-24; 12:34; 14:25; Luke 4:43; 6:20; 7:28; 8:10; 9:27,60,62; 10:9-11; 11:20; 13:18,20,28-29; 17:20-21; 18:16-17,24-25,29; 21:31; 22:16,18; John 3:3,5.*

LAST SUPPER

Luke 22:15-18, ✥ ¹⁵"I have eagerly desired to eat this Passover with you before I suffer. ¹⁶For I tell you, I will not eat it again until it finds fulfillment in the kingdom of God…¹⁷Take this and divide it among you. ¹⁸For I tell you I will not drink again of the fruit of the vine until the kingdom of God comes."

See also *Matthew 26:26-29; Mark 14:22,24-25; 1 Corinthians 11:24-25.*

LAZARUS

John 11:4,7,9-11,14-15,23,25-26,34,39-44

⁴"This sickness will not end in death. No, it is for God's glory so that God's Son may be glorified through it…⁷Let us go back to Judea…⁹Are there not twelve hours of daylight? A man who walks by day will not stumble, for he sees by this world's light. ¹⁰It is when he walks by night that he stumbles, for he has no light. ¹¹…Our friend Lazarus has fallen asleep; but I am going there to wake him up…¹⁴Lazarus is dead, ¹⁵and for your sake I am glad I was not there, so that you may believe. But let us go to him…²³Your brother will rise again…²⁵I am the resurrection and the life. He who believes in me will live, even though he dies; ²⁶and whoever lives and believes in me will

never die. Do you believe this?…³⁴Where have you laid him?…³⁹Take away the stone. ⁴⁰Did I not tell you that if you believed, you would see the glory of God? ⁴¹…Father, I thank you that you have heard me. ⁴²I knew that you always hear me, but I said this for the benefit of the people standing here, that they may believe that you sent me. ⁴³…Lazarus, come out! ⁴⁴…Take off the grave clothes and let him go."

LETTERS TO THE CHURCHES

Letter to the Church at Ephesus

Revelation 2:1-7 ¹"To the angel of the church in Ephesus write: These are the words of him who holds the seven stars in his right hand and walks among the seven golden lampstands: ²I know your deeds, your hard work and your perseverance. I know that you cannot tolerate wicked men, that you have tested those who claim to be apostles but are not, and have found them false. ³You have persevered and have endured hardships for my name, and have not grown weary. ⁴Yet I hold this against you: You have forsaken your first love. ⁵Remember the height from which you have fallen! Repent and do the things you did at first. If you do not repent, I will come to you and remove your lampstand from its place. ⁶But you have this in your favor: You hate the practices of the Nicolaitans, which I also hate. ⁷He who has an ear, let him hear what the Spirit says to the churches. To him who overcomes, I will give the right to eat from the tree of life, which is in the paradise of God."

Letter to the Church at Smyrna

Revelation 2:8-10 ⟨⟨⟨ ⁸"These are the words of him who is the First and the Last, who died and came to life again. ⁹I know your afflictions and your poverty—yet you are rich! I know the slander of those who say they are Jews and are not, but are a synagogue of Satan. ¹⁰Do not be afraid of what you are about to suffer. I tell you, the devil will put some of you in prison to test you, and you will suffer persecution for ten days. Be faithful, even to the point of death, and I will give you the crown of life."

Letter to the Church at Pergamum

Revelation 2:12-16 12"To the angel of the church in Pergamum write: These are the words of him who has the sharp, double-edged sword. 13I know where you live—where Satan has his throne. Yet you remain true to my name. You did not renounce your faith in me, even in the days of Antipas, my faithful witness, who was put to death in your city—where Satan lives. 14Nevertheless, I have a few things against you: You have people there who hold to the teaching of Balaam, who taught Balak to entice the Israelites to sin by eating food sacrificed to idols and by committing sexual immorality. 15Likewise you also have those who hold to the teaching of the Nicolaitans. 16Repent therefore! Otherwise, I will soon come to you and will fight against them with the sword of my mouth."

Letter to the Church at Thyatira

Revelation 2:18-25 18"To the angel of the church in Thyatira write: These are the words of the Son of God, whose eyes are like blazing fire and whose feet are like burnished bronze. 19I know your deeds, your love and faith, your service and perseverance, and that you are now doing more than you did at first. [20]Nevertheless, I have this against you: You tolerate that woman Jezebel, who calls herself a prophetess. By her teaching she misleads my servants into sexual immorality and the eating of food sacrificed to idols. [21]I have given her time to repent of her immorality, but she is unwilling. [22]So I will cast her on a bed of suffering, and I will make those who commit adultery with her suffer intensely, unless they repent of her ways. [23]I will strike her children dead. Then all the churches will know that I am he who searches hearts and minds, and I will repay each of you according to your deeds. [24]Now I say to the rest of you in Thyatira, to you who do not hold to her teaching and have not learned Satan's so-called deep secrets (I will not impose any other burden on you): [25]Only hold on to what you have until I come."

Letter to the Church at Sardis

Revelation 3:1-4 [1]"To the angel of the church in Sardis write: These are the words of him who holds the seven spirits of God and the seven stars. I know your deeds; you have a reputation of being alive, but you are dead. ²Wake up! Strengthen what remains and is about to die, for I have not found your deeds complete in the sight of my God. ³Remember, therefore, what you have received and heard; obey it, and repent. But if you do not wake up, I will come like a thief, and you will not know at what time I will come to you. ⁴Yet you have a few people in Sardis who have not soiled their clothes. They will walk with me, dressed in white, for they are worthy."

Letter to the Church at Philadelphia

Revelation 3:7-11 ⌒⌒⌒ ⁷"To the angel of the church in Philadelphia write: These are the words of him who is holy and true, who holds the key of David. What he opens no one can shut, and what he shuts no one can open. ⁸I know your deeds. See, I have placed before you an open door that no one can shut. I know that you have little strength, yet you have kept my word and have not denied my name. ⁹I will make those who are of the synagogue of Satan, who claim to be Jews though they are not, but are liars—I will make them come and fall down at your feet and acknowledge that I have loved you. ¹⁰Since you have kept my command to endure patiently, I will also keep you from the hour of trial that is going to come upon the whole world to test those who live on the earth. ¹¹I am coming soon. Hold on to what you have, so that no one will take your crown."

Letter to the Church at Laodicea

Revelation 3:14-20 ⟨∞⟩ ¹⁴"To the angel of the church in Laodicea write: These are the words of the Amen, the faithful and true witness, the ruler of God's creation. ¹⁵I know your deeds, that you are neither cold nor hot. I wish you were either one or the other! ¹⁶So, because you are lukewarm—neither hot nor cold—I am about to spit you out of my mouth. ¹⁷You say, 'I am rich; I have acquired wealth and do not need a thing.' But you do not realize that you are wretched, pitiful, poor, blind and naked. ¹⁸I counsel you to buy from me gold refined in the fire, so you can become rich; and white clothes to wear, so you can cover your shameful nakedness; and salve to put on your eyes, so you can see. ¹⁹Those whom

I love I rebuke and discipline. So be earnest, and repent. [20] Here I am! I stand at the door and knock. If anyone hears my voice and opens the door, I will come in and eat with him, and he with me."

See also *Revelation 1:8,11,17-20; 2:11,17,26-29; 3:5-6,12-13,21-22*.

LIGHT

Mark 4:21-25 [21]"Do you bring in a lamp to put it under a bowl or a bed? Instead, don't you put it on its stand? [22]For whatever is hidden is meant to be disclosed, and whatever is concealed is meant to be brought out into the open. [23]If anyone has ears to hear, let him hear. [24]Consider carefully what you hear...With the measure you use, it will be measured to you—and even more. [25]Whoever has will be given more; whoever does not have, even what he has will be taken from him."

John 9:3-5 [3]"Neither this man nor his parents sinned...but this happened so that the work of God might be displayed in his life. [4]As long as it is day, we must do the work of him who sent me.

Night is coming, when no one can work. ⁵While I am in the world, I am the light of the world."

See also *Matthew 5:13-16; 6:22-23; Luke 8:16-18; 11:33-36; John 8:12.*

LIVING WATER

John 4:10,13-14 🙖 ¹⁰"If you knew the gift of God and who it is that asks you for a drink, you would have asked him and he would have given you living water...¹³Everyone who drinks this water will be thirsty again, ¹⁴but whoever drinks the water I give him will never thirst. Indeed, the water I give him will become in him a spring of water welling up to eternal life."

See also *John 7:37-38.*

LOVE

Matthew 5:43-48 🙖 ⁴³"You have heard that it was said, 'Love your neighbor and hate your enemy.' ⁴⁴But I tell you: Love your enemies and pray for those who persecute you, ⁴⁵that you may be sons of your Father in heaven. He causes his sun to rise on the evil and the good, and sends rain on the righteous and the unrighteous. ⁴⁶If you love those who love you, what reward will you get? Are not even the tax collectors doing that? ⁴⁷And if you greet only your brothers, what are you doing more than others? Do not even pagans do that? ⁴⁸Be perfect, therefore, as your heavenly Father is perfect."

Matthew 7:12 ⁱ²"So in everything, do to others what you would have them do to you, for this sums up the Law and the Prophets."

Matthew 22:37-40 ³⁷"'Love the Lord your God with all your heart and with all your soul and with all your mind.' ³⁸This is the first and greatest commandment. ³⁹And the second is like it: 'Love your neighbor as yourself.' ⁴⁰All the Law and the Prophets hang on these two commandments."

John 13:34-35 ³⁴"A new command I give you: Love one another. As I have loved you, so you must love one another. ³⁵By this all men will know that you are my disciples, if you love one another."

See also *Matthew 22:37-40; Mark 12:29-31; Luke 6:27-36; John 15:17.*

MERCY

Matthew 9:12-13 ⟨∞⟩ 12"It is not the healthy who need a doctor, but the sick. 13But go and learn what this means: 'I desire mercy, not sacrifice.' For I have not come to call the righteous, but sinners."

Matthew 12:7 ⟨∞⟩ 7"If you had known what these words mean, 'I desire mercy, not sacrifice,' you would not have condemned the innocent."

See also *Luke 5:31-32*.

MIRACLES

Matthew 15:32,34 ⟨∞⟩ 32"I have compassion for these people; they have already been with me three days and have nothing to eat. I do not want to send them away hungry, or they may collapse on the way...34How many loaves do you have?"

John 2:4 ⟨∞⟩ 4 [In response to his mother's comment that there is no wine at the wedding at Cana] "Woman, what does that have to do with us? My hour has not yet come." [After this his mother tells the servants to do whatever he tells them, and Jesus turns water into wine.]

See also *Matthew 14:16,18; Mark 6:37-38; Luke 4:23-27; 9:13-14; John 2:7,8; John 6:5,10,12.*

MONEY

Matthew 6:24 ²⁴"No one can serve two masters; for either he will hate the one and love the other, or he will be devoted to one and despise the other. You cannot serve God and wealth."

See also *Luke 16:13.*

OBEDIENCE

Luke 8:21 ²¹"My mother and brothers are those who hear God's word and put it into practice."

John 15:9-16 ⁹"As the Father has loved me, so have I loved you. Now remain in my love. ¹⁰ If you obey my commands, you will remain in my love, just as I have obeyed my Father's commands and remain in his love. ¹¹I have told you this so that my joy may be in you and that your joy may be complete. ¹²My command is this: Love each other as I have loved you. ¹³Greater love has no one than this, that he lay down his life for his friends. ¹⁴You are my friends if you do what I command. ¹⁵I no longer call you servants, because a servant does not know his master's business. Instead, I have called you friends, for everything that I learned from my Father I have made known to you. ¹⁶You did not choose me, but I chose you and appointed you to go and bear fruit—fruit that will last. Then the Father will give you whatever you ask in my name."

See also *Luke 11:28; John 14:15,21,23-24; 15:17.*

OVERCOMING

John 16:32 ³²"But a time is coming, and has come, when you will be scattered, each to his own home. You will leave me all alone. Yet I am not alone, for my Father is with me."

See also *John 16:25-28,31,33.*

PARABLES

Fig Tree

Luke 13:6-9 ⁶"A man had a fig tree, planted in his vineyard, and he went to look for fruit on it, but did not find any. ⁷So he said to the man who took care of the vineyard, 'For three years now

I've been coming to look for fruit on this fig tree and haven't found any. Cut it down! Why should it use up the soil?' ⁸'Sir,' the man replied, 'leave it alone for one more year, and I'll dig around it and fertilize it. ⁹ If it bears fruit next year, fine! If not, then cut it down.'"

Friend at Midnight

Luke 11:5-8 ⁵"Suppose one of you has a friend, and he goes to him at midnight and says, 'Friend, lend me three loaves of bread, ⁶because a friend of mine on a journey has come to me, and I have nothing to set before him.' ⁷Then the one inside answers, 'Don't bother me. The door is already locked, and my children are with me in bed. I can't get up and give you anything.' ⁸I tell you, though he will not get up and give him the bread because he is his friend, yet because of the man's boldness he will get up and give him as much as he needs."

Good Samaritan

Luke 10: 26,28,30-37 ²⁶"What is written in the Law?...How do you read it?...²⁸You have answered correctly. Do this and live…³⁰A man was going down from Jerusalem to Jericho, when he fell into the hands of robbers. They stripped him of his clothes, beat him and went away, leaving him half dead. ³¹A priest happened to be going down the same road, and when he saw the man, he passed by on the other side. ³²So too, a Levite, when he came to the place and saw him, passed by on the other side. ³³But a Samaritan, as he traveled, came where the man was; and when he saw him, he took pity on him. ³⁴He went to him and bandaged his wounds, pouring on oil and wine. Then he put the man on his own donkey, took him to an inn and took care of him. ³⁵The next day he took out two silver coins and gave them to the innkeeper. 'Look after him,' he said, 'and when I return, I will reimburse you for any extra expense you may have.' ³⁶Which of these three do you think was a neighbor to the man who fell into the hands of robbers? ³⁷Go and do likewise."

Great Supper

Luke 14:16-24 ❧ ¹⁶"A certain man was preparing a great banquet and invited many guests. ¹⁷At the time of the banquet he sent his servant to tell those who had been invited, 'Come, for everything is now ready.' ¹⁸But they all alike began to make excuses. The first said, 'I have just bought a field, and I must go and see it. Please excuse me.' ¹⁹Another said, 'I have just bought five yoke of oxen, and I'm on my way to try them out. Please excuse me.' ²⁰Still another said, 'I just got married, so I can't come.' ²¹The servant came back and reported this to his master. Then the owner of the house became angry and ordered his servant, 'Go out quickly into the streets and alleys of the town and bring in the poor, the crippled, the blind and the lame.' ²²'Sir,' the servant said, 'what you ordered has been done, but there is still room.' ²³Then the master told his servant, 'Go out to the roads and country lanes and make them come in, so that my house will be full. ²⁴I tell you, not one of those men who were invited will get a taste of my banquet.'"

Lost Coin

Luke 15:8-10 ⁸"Or suppose a woman has ten silver coins and loses one. Does she not light a lamp, sweep the house and search carefully until she finds it? ⁹And when she finds it, she calls her friends and neighbors together and says, 'Rejoice with me; I have found my lost coin.' ¹⁰ In the same way, I tell you, there is rejoicing in the presence of the angels of God over one sinner who repents."

Lost Sheep

Matthew 18:12-14 ⁽ᵉᵍ⁾ ¹²"What do you think? If a man owns a hundred sheep, and one of them wanders away, will he not leave the ninety-nine on the hills and go to look for the one that wandered off? ¹³And if he finds it, I tell you the truth, he is happier about that one sheep than about the ninety-nine that did not wander off. ¹⁴In the same way your Father in heaven is not willing that any of these little ones should be lost."

Luke 15:4-7 ⁽ᵉᵍ⁾ ⁴"Suppose one of you has a hundred sheep and loses one of them. Does he not leave the ninety-nine in the open country and go after the lost sheep until he finds it? ⁵And when he finds it, he joyfully puts it on his shoulders ⁶and goes home. Then he calls his friends and neighbors together and says, 'Rejoice with me; I have found my lost sheep.' ⁷I tell you that in the same way there will be more rejoicing in heaven over one sinner who repents than over ninety-nine righteous persons who do not need to repent."

Lost Son

Luke 15:11-32 ⟶ ¹¹"There was a man who had two sons. ¹²The younger one said to his father, 'Father, give me my share of the estate.' So he divided his property between them. ¹³Not long after that, the younger son got together all he had, set off for a distant country and there squandered his wealth in wild living. ¹⁴After he had spent everything, there was a severe famine in that whole country, and he began to be in need. ¹⁵So he went and hired himself out to a citizen of that country, who sent him to his fields to feed pigs. ¹⁶He longed to fill his stomach with the pods that the pigs were eating, but no one gave him anything. ¹⁷When he came to his senses, he said, 'How many of my father's hired men have food to spare, and here I am starving to death! ¹⁸I will set out and go back to my father and say to him: Father, I have sinned against heaven and against you. [19]I am no longer worthy to be called your son; make me like one of your hired men.' [20]So he got up and went to his father. But while he was still a long way off, his father saw him and was filled with compassion for him; he ran to his son, threw his arms around him and kissed him. [21]The son said to him, 'Father, I have sinned against heaven and against you. I am no longer worthy to be called your son.' [22]But the father said to his servants, 'Quick! Bring the best robe and put it on him. Put a ring on his finger and sandals on his feet. [23]Bring the fattened calf and kill it. Let's have a feast and celebrate. [24]For this son of mine was dead and is alive again; he was lost and is found.' So they began to celebrate. [25]Meanwhile, the older son was in the field. When he came near the house, he heard music and dancing. [26]So he called one of the servants and asked him what was going on. [27]'Your brother has come,' he replied, 'and your father has killed the fattened calf because he has him back safe and sound.' [28]The older brother became angry and refused to go in. So his father went out and pleaded with him. [29]But he answered his father,

'Look! All these years I've been slaving for you and never disobeyed your orders. Yet you never gave me even a young goat so I could celebrate with my friends. ³⁰But when this son of yours who has squandered your property with prostitutes comes home, you kill the fattened calf for him!' ³¹'My son,' the father said, 'you are always with me, and everything I have is yours. ³²But we had to celebrate and be glad, because this brother of yours was dead and is alive again; he was lost and is found.'"

Mustard Seed

Matthew 13:31-32 ³¹"The kingdom of heaven is like a mustard seed, which a man took and planted in his field. ³²Though it is the smallest of all your seeds, yet when it grows, it is the largest of garden plants and becomes a tree, so that the birds of the air come and perch in its branches."

Mark 4:30-32 ³⁰"What shall we say the kingdom of God is like, or what parable shall we use to describe it? ³¹It is like a mustard seed, which is the smallest seed you plant in the ground. ³²Yet when planted, it grows and becomes the largest of all garden plants, with such big branches that the birds of the air can perch in its shade."

Luke 13:18-19 ◦ [18]"What is the kingdom of God like? What shall I compare it to? [19]It is like a mustard seed, which a man took and planted in his garden. It grew and became a tree, and the birds of the air perched in its branches."

Net

Matthew 13:47-52 ◦ [47]"Once again, the kingdom of heaven is like a net that was let down into the lake and caught all kinds of fish. [48]When it was full, the fishermen pulled it up on the shore. Then they sat down and collected the good fish in baskets, but threw the bad away. [49]This is how it will be at the end of the age. The angels will come and separate the wicked from the righteous [50]and throw them into the fiery furnace, where there will be weeping and gnashing of teeth. [51]Have you understood all these things?...[52]Therefore every teacher of the law who has been instructed about the kingdom of heaven is like the owner of a house who brings out of his storeroom new treasures as well as old."

Pearl

Matthew 13:45-46 **45**"Again, the kingdom of heaven is like a merchant looking for fine pearls. **46**When he found one of great value, he went away and sold everything he had and bought it."

Persistent Widow

Luke 18:2-8 **2**"In a certain town there was a judge who neither feared God nor cared about men. **3**And there was a widow in that town who kept coming to him with the plea, 'Grant me justice against my adversary.' **4**For some time he refused. But finally he said to himself, 'Even though I don't fear God or care about men, **5**yet because this widow keeps bothering me, I will see that she gets justice, so that she won't eventually wear me out with her coming!' **6**Listen to what the unjust judge says. **7**And will not God bring about justice for his chosen ones, who cry out to him day and night? Will he keep putting them off? **8**I tell you, he will see that they get justice, and quickly. However, when the Son of Man comes, will he find faith on the earth?"

Pharisee and Tax Collector

Luke 18:10-14 ¹⁰"Two men went up to the temple to pray, one a Pharisee and the other a tax collector. ¹¹The Pharisee stood up and prayed about himself: 'God, I thank you that I am not like other men—robbers, evildoers, adulterers—or even like this tax collector. ¹²I fast twice a week and give a tenth of all I get.' ¹³But the tax collector stood at a distance. He would not even look up to heaven, but beat his breast and said, 'God, have mercy on me, a sinner.' ¹⁴I tell you that this man, rather than the other, went home justified before God. For everyone who exalts himself will be humbled, and he who humbles himself will be exalted."

Rich Fool

Luke 12:14-21 ¹⁴"Man, who appointed me a judge or an arbiter between you? ¹⁵Watch out! Be on your guard against all kinds of greed; a man's life does not consist in the abundance of his possessions. ¹⁶The ground of a certain rich man produced a good crop. ¹⁷He thought to him-self, 'What shall I do? I have no place to store my crops.' ¹⁸Then he said, 'This is what I'll do. I will tear down my barns and build bigger ones, and there I will store all my grain and my goods. ¹⁹And I'll say to myself, "You have plenty of good things laid up for many years. Take life easy; eat, drink and be merry."' ²⁰But God said to him, 'You fool! This very night your life will be demanded from you. Then who will get what you have prepared for yourself?' ²¹This is how it will be with anyone who stores up things for himself but is not rich toward God."

Rich Man and Lazarus

Luke 16:19-31 ⮕ ¹⁹"There was a rich man who was dressed in purple and fine linen and lived in luxury every day. ²⁰At his gate was laid a beggar named Lazarus, covered with sores ²¹and longing to eat what fell from the rich man's table. Even the dogs came and licked his sores. ²²The time came when the beggar died and the angels carried him to Abraham's side. The rich man also died and was buried. ²³In hell, where he was in torment, he looked up and saw Abraham far away, with Lazarus by his side. ²⁴So he called to him, 'Father Abraham, have pity on me and send

Lazarus to dip the tip of his finger in water and cool my tongue, because I am in agony in this fire.' ²⁵But Abraham replied, 'Son, remember that in your lifetime you received your good things, while Lazarus received bad things, but now he is comforted here and you are in agony. ²⁶And besides all this, between us and you a great chasm has been fixed, so that those who want to go from here to you cannot, nor can anyone cross over from there to us.' ²⁷He answered, 'Then I beg you, father, send Lazarus to my father's house, ²⁸for I have five brothers. Let him warn them, so that they will not also come to this place of torment.' ²⁹Abraham replied, 'They have Moses and the Prophets; let them listen to them.' ³⁰'No, father Abraham,' he said, 'but if someone from the dead goes to them, they will repent.' ³¹He said to him, 'If they do not listen to Moses and the Prophets, they will not be convinced even if someone rises from the dead.'"

Seed

Mark 4:26-29 ²⁶"This is what the kingdom of God is like. A man scatters seed on the ground. ²⁷Night and day, whether he sleeps or gets up, the seed sprouts and grows, though he does not know how. ²⁸All by itself the soil produces grain—first the stalk, then the head, then the full kernel in the head. ²⁹As soon as the grain is ripe, he puts the sickle to it, because the harvest has come."

Shrewd Manager

Luke 16:1-13 ¹"There was a rich man whose manager was accused of wasting his possessions. ²So he called him in and asked him, 'What is this I hear about you? Give an account of your management, because you cannot be manager any longer.' ³The manager said to himself, 'What shall I do now? My master is taking away my job. I'm not strong enough to dig, and I'm ashamed to beg—⁴I know what I'll do so that, when I lose my job here, people will welcome me into their houses.' ⁵So he called in each one of his master's debtors. He asked the first, 'How much do you owe my master?' ⁶'Eight hundred gallons of olive oil,' he replied. The manager told him, 'Take your bill, sit down quickly, and make it four hundred.' ⁷Then he asked the second, 'And how much do you owe?' 'A thousand bushels of wheat,' he replied.

He told him, 'Take your bill and make it eight hundred.' [8]The master commended the dishonest manager because he had acted shrewdly. For the people of this world are more shrewd in dealing with their own kind than are the people of the light. [9]I tell you, use worldly wealth to gain friends for yourselves, so that when it is gone, you will be welcomed into eternal dwellings. [10]Whoever can be trusted with very little can also be trusted with much, and whoever is dishonest with very little will also be dishonest with much. [11]So if you have not been trustworthy in handling worldly wealth, who will trust you with true riches? [12]And if you have not been trustworthy with someone else's property, who will give you property of your own? [13]No servant can serve two masters. Either he will hate the one and love the other, or he will be devoted to the one and despise the other. You cannot serve both God and Money."

Sower

Matthew 13:3-9,11-23 ✐ [3]"A farmer went out to sow his seed. [4]As he was scattering the seed, some fell along the path, and the birds came and ate it up. ⁵Some fell on rocky places, where it did not have much soil. It sprang up quickly, because the soil was shallow. ⁶But when the sun came up, the plants were scorched, and they withered because they had no root. ⁷Other seed fell among thorns, which grew up and choked the plants. ⁸Still other seed fell on good soil, where it produced a crop—a hundred, sixty or thirty times what was sown. ⁹He who has ears, let him hear...¹¹The knowledge of the secrets of the kingdom of heaven has been given to you, but not to them. ¹²Whoever has will be given more, and he will have an abundance. Whoever does not have, even what he has will be taken from him. ¹³This is why I speak to them in parables: Though seeing, they do not see; though hearing, they do not hear or understand. ¹⁴In them is fulfilled the prophecy of Isaiah: 'You will be ever hearing but never understanding; you will be ever seeing but never perceiving. ¹⁵For this people's heart has become calloused; they hardly hear with their ears, and they have closed their eyes. Otherwise they might see with their eyes, hear with their ears, understand with their hearts and turn, and I would heal them.' ¹⁶But blessed are your eyes because they see, and your ears because they hear. ¹⁷For I tell you the truth, many prophets and righteous men longed to see what you see but did not see it, and to hear what you hear but did not hear it. ¹⁸Listen then to what the parable of the sower means: ¹⁹When anyone hears the message about the kingdom and does not understand it, the evil one comes and snatches away what was sown in his heart. This is the seed sown along the path. ²⁰The one who received the seed that fell on rocky places is the man who hears the word and at once receives it with joy. ²¹But since he has no root, he lasts only a short time. When trouble or persecution comes because of the word, he quickly falls away. ²²The one who received the seed that fell among the thorns is the man who hears the word, but the worries of this life and the deceitfulness of wealth choke it, making it unfruitful. ²³But the one who received the seed that fell on good soil is the man who hears the word and understands it. He produces a crop, yielding a hundred, sixty or thirty times what was sown."

See also *Mark 4:3-9,11-20; Luke 8:5-8,10-15.*

Talents

Matthew 25:14-30 ⨀ [14]"Again, it will be like a man going on a journey, who called his servants and entrusted his property to them. [15]To one he gave five talents of money, to another two talents, and to another one talent, each according to his ability. Then he went on his journey. [16]The man who had received the five talents went at once and put his money to work and gained five more. [17]So also, the one with the two talents gained two more. [18]But the man who had received the one talent went off, dug a hole in the ground and hid his master's money. [19]After a long time the master of those servants returned and settled accounts with them. [20]The man who had received the five talents brought the other five. 'Master,' he said, 'you entrusted me with five talents. See, I have gained five more.' [21]His master replied, 'Well done, good and faithful servant! You have been faithful with a few things; I will put you in charge of many things. Come and share your master's happiness!' [22]The man with the two talents also came. 'Master,' he said, 'you entrusted me with two talents; see, I have gained two more.' ²³His master replied, 'Well done, good and faithful servant! You have been faithful with a few things; I will put you in charge of many things. Come and share your master's happiness!' ²⁴Then the man who had received the one talent came. 'Master,' he said, 'I knew that you are a hard man, harvesting where you have not sown and gathering where you have not scattered seed. ²⁵So I was afraid and went out and hid your talent in the ground. See, here is what belongs to you.' ²⁶His master replied, 'You wicked, lazy servant! So you knew that I harvest where I have not sown and gather where I have not scattered seed? ²⁷Well then, you should have put my money on deposit with the bankers, so that when I returned I would have received it back with interest. ²⁸Take the talent from him and give it to the one who has the ten talents. ²⁹For everyone who has will be given more, and he will have an abundance. Whoever does not have, even what he has will be taken from him. ³⁰And throw that worthless servant outside, into the darkness, where there will be weeping and gnashing of teeth.'"

Ten Servants Given Ten Minas

Luke 19:12-27 ~ [12]"A man of noble birth went to a distant country to have himself appointed king and then to return. [13]So he called ten of his servants and gave them ten minas. 'Put this money to work,' he said, 'until I come back.' [14]But his subjects hated him and sent a delegation after him to say, 'We don't want this man to be our king.' [15]He was made king, however, and returned home. Then he sent for the servants to whom he had given the money, in order to find out what they had gained with it. [16]The first one came and said, 'Sir, your mina has earned ten more.' [17]'Well done, my good servant!' his master replied. 'Because you have been trustworthy in a very small matter, take charge of ten cities.' [18]The second came and said, 'Sir, your mina has earned five more.' [19]His master answered, 'You take charge of five cities.' [20]Then another servant came and said, 'Sir, here is your mina; I have kept it laid away in a piece of cloth. [21]I was afraid of you, because you are a hard man. You take out what you did not put in and reap what you did not sow.' [22]His master replied, 'I will judge you by your own words, you wicked servant! You knew, did you, that I am a hard man, taking out what I did not put in, and reaping what I did not sow? ²³Why then didn't you put my money on deposit, so that when I came back, I could have collected it with interest?' ²⁴Then he said to those standing by, 'Take his mina away from him and give it to the one who has ten minas.' ²⁵'Sir,' they said, 'he already has ten!' ²⁶He replied, 'I tell you that to everyone who has, more will be given, but as for the one who has nothing, what he has will be taken away. ²⁷But those enemies of mine who did not want me to be king over them—bring them here and kill them in front of me.'"

Treasure

Matthew 13:44 ⁴⁴"The kingdom of heaven is like treasure hidden in a field. When a man found it, he hid it again, and then in his joy went and sold all he had and bought that field."

Two Debtors

Luke 7:41-42 ⁴¹"Two men owed money to a certain moneylender. One owed him five hundred denarii, and the other fifty. ⁴²Neither of them had the money to pay him back, so he canceled the debts of both. Now which of them will love him more?"

Two Sons

Matthew 21:28-32 ²⁸"What do you think? There was a man who had two sons. He went to the first and said, 'Son, go and work today in the vineyard.' ²⁹'I will not,' he answered, but later he changed his mind and went. ³⁰Then the father went to the other son and said the same thing. He answered, 'I will, sir,' but he did not go. ³¹Which of the two did what his father wanted? I tell you the truth, the tax collectors and the prostitutes are entering the kingdom of God ahead of you. ³²For John came to you to show you the way of righteousness, and you did not believe him, but the tax collectors and the prostitutes did. And even after you saw this, you did not repent and believe him."

Unmerciful Servant

Matthew 18:23-35 ²³"Therefore, the kingdom of heaven is like a king who wanted to settle accounts with his servants. ²⁴As he began the settlement, a man who owed him ten thousand talents was brought to him. ²⁵Since he was not able to pay, the master ordered that he and his wife and his children and all that he had be sold to repay the debt. ²⁶The servant fell on his knees before him. 'Be patient with me,' he begged, 'and I will pay back everything.' ²⁷The servant's master took pity on him, canceled the debt and let him go. ²⁸But when that servant went out, he found one of his fellow servants who owed him a hundred denarii. He grabbed him and began to choke him. 'Pay back what you owe me!' he demanded. ²⁹His fellow servant fell to his knees and begged him, 'Be patient with me, and I will pay you back.' ³⁰But he refused. Instead, he went off and had the man thrown into prison until he could pay the debt. ³¹When the other servants saw what had happened, they were greatly distressed and went and told their master everything that had happened. ³²Then the master called the servant in. 'You wicked servant,' he said, 'I canceled all that debt of yours because you begged me to. ³³Shouldn't you have had mercy on your fellow servant just as I had on you?' ³⁴In anger his master turned him over to the jailers to be tortured, until he should pay back all he owed. ³⁵This is how my heavenly Father will treat each of you unless you forgive your brother from your heart."

Workers in the Vineyard

Matthew 20:1-16 ¹"For the kingdom of heaven is like a landowner who went out early in the morning to hire men to work in his vineyard. ²He agreed to pay them a denarius for the day and sent them into his vineyard. ³About the third hour he went out and saw others standing in the marketplace doing nothing. ⁴He told them, 'You also go and work in my vineyard, and I will pay you whatever is right.' ⁵So they went. He went out again about the sixth hour and the ninth hour and did the same thing. ⁶About the eleventh hour he went out and found still others standing around. He asked them, 'Why have you been standing here all day long doing nothing?' ⁷'Because no one has hired us,' they answered. He said to them, 'You also go and work in my vineyard.' ⁸When evening came, the owner of the vineyard said to his foreman, 'Call the workers and pay them their wages, beginning with the last ones hired and going on to the first.' ⁹The workers who were hired about the eleventh hour came and each received a denarius. ¹⁰So when those came who were hired first, they expected to receive more. But each one of them also received a denarius. ¹¹When they received it, they began to grumble against the landowner. ¹²'These men who were hired last worked only one hour,' they said, 'and you have made them equal to us who have borne the burden of the work and the heat of the day.' ¹³But he answered one of them, 'Friend, I am not being unfair to you. Didn't you agree to work for a denarius? ¹⁴Take your pay and go. I want to give the man who was hired last the same as I gave you. ¹⁵Don't I have the right to do what I want with my own money? Or are you envious because I am generous?' ¹⁶So the last will be first, and the first will be last."

Virgins

Matthew 25:1-13 ✎ ¹"At that time the kingdom of heaven will be like ten virgins who took their lamps and went out to meet the bridegroom. [2]Five of them were foolish and five were wise. [3]The foolish ones took their lamps but did not take any oil with them. [4]The wise, however, took oil in jars along with their lamps. [5]The bridegroom was a long time in coming, and they all became drowsy and fell asleep. [6]At midnight the cry rang out: 'Here's the bridegroom! Come out to meet him!' [7]Then all the virgins woke up and trimmed their lamps. [8]The foolish ones said to the wise, 'Give us some of your oil; our lamps are going out.' [9]'No,' they replied, 'there may not be enough for both us and you. Instead, go to those who sell oil and buy some for yourselves.' [10]But while they were on their way to buy the oil, the bridegroom arrived. The virgins who were ready went in with him to the wedding banquet. And the door was shut. [11]Later the others also came. 'Sir! Sir!' they said. 'Open the door for us!' [12]But he replied, 'I tell you the truth, I don't know you.' [13]Therefore keep watch, because you do not know the day or the hour."

Wedding

Matthew 22:2-14 ⟳ ²"The kingdom of heaven is like a king who prepared a wedding banquet for his son. ³He sent his servants to those who had been invited to the banquet to tell them to come, but they refused to come. ⁴Then he sent some more servants and said, 'Tell those who have been invited that I have prepared my dinner: My oxen and fattened cattle have been butchered, and everything is ready. Come to the wedding banquet.' ⁵But they paid no attention and went off—one to his field, another to his business. ⁶The rest seized his servants, mistreated them and killed them. ⁷The king was enraged. He sent his army and destroyed those murderers and burned their city. ⁸Then he said to his servants, 'The wedding banquet is ready, but those I invited did not deserve to come. ⁹Go to the street corners and invite to the banquet anyone you find.' ¹⁰So the servants went out into the streets and gathered all the people they could find, both good and bad, and the wedding hall was filled with guests. ¹¹But when the king came in to see the guests, he noticed a

man there who was not wearing wedding clothes.
¹²'Friend,' he asked, 'how did you get in here without wedding clothes?' The man was speechless.
¹³Then the king told the attendants, 'Tie him hand and foot, and throw him outside, into the darkness, where there will be weeping and gnashing of teeth.'
¹⁴For many are invited, but few are chosen."

Weeds

Matthew 13:24-30,37-43 ²⁴"The kingdom of heaven is like a man who sowed good seed in his field. ²⁵But while everyone was sleeping, his enemy came and sowed weeds among the wheat, and went away. ²⁶When the wheat sprouted and formed heads, then the weeds also appeared. ²⁷The owner's servants came to him and said, 'Sir, didn't you sow good seed in your field? Where then did the weeds come from?' ²⁸'An enemy did this,' he replied. The servants asked him, 'Do you want us to go and pull them up?' ²⁹'No,' he answered, 'because while you are pulling the weeds, you may root up the wheat with them. ³⁰Let both grow together until the harvest. At that time I will tell the harvesters: First collect the weeds and tie them in bundles to be burned; then gather the wheat and bring it into my barn'...³⁷The one who sowed the good seed is the Son of Man. ³⁸The field is the world, and the good seed stands for the sons of the kingdom. The weeds are the sons of the evil one, ³⁹and the enemy who sows them is the devil. The harvest is the end of the age, and the harvesters are angels. ⁴⁰As the weeds are pulled up and burned in the fire, so it will be at the end of the age. ⁴¹The Son of Man will send out his angels, and they will weed out of his kingdom everything that causes sin and all who do evil. ⁴²They will throw them into the fiery furnace, where there will be weeping and gnashing of teeth. ⁴³Then the righteous will shine like the sun in the kingdom of their Father. He who has ears, let him hear."

Wicked Tenants

Matthew 21:33-40,42-44 ⟶ ³³"Listen to another parable: There was a landowner who planted a vineyard. He put a wall around it, dug a winepress in it and built a watchtower. Then he rented the vineyard to some farmers and went away on a journey. ³⁴When the harvest time approached, he sent his servants to the tenants to collect his fruit. ³⁵The tenants seized his servants; they beat one, killed another, and stoned a third. ³⁶Then he sent other servants to them, more than the first time, and the tenants treated them the same way. ³⁷Last of all, he sent his son to them. 'They will respect my son,' he said. ³⁸But when the tenants saw the son, they said to each other, 'This is the heir. Come, let's kill him and take his inheritance.' ³⁹So they took him and threw him out of the vineyard and killed him. ⁴⁰Therefore, when the owner of the vineyard comes, what will he do to those tenants?... ⁴²Have you never read in the scriptures: 'The stone the builders rejected has become the capstone; the Lord has done this, and it is marvelous in our eyes'? ⁴³Therefore I tell you that the kingdom of God will be taken away from you and given to a people who will produce its fruit. ⁴⁴He who falls on this stone will be broken to pieces, but he on whom it falls will be crushed."

See also *Mark 12:1-11; Luke 20:9-18.*

Yeast

Luke 13:20-21 ❦ ²⁰"What shall I compare the kingdom of God to? ²¹It is like yeast that a woman took and mixed into a large amount of flour until it worked all through the dough."

See also *Matthew 13:33*.

PAUL (SAUL)

Acts 9:4-6,10-12,15-16 ❦ ⁴"Saul, Saul, why do you persecute me? ⁵I am Jesus, whom you are persecuting. ⁶Now get up and go into the city, and you will be told what you must do…¹⁰Ananias! ¹¹Go to the house of Judas on Straight Street and ask for a man from Tarsus named Saul, for he is praying. ¹²In a vision he has seen a man named Ananias come and place his hands on him to restore his sight…¹⁵Go! This man is my chosen instrument to carry my name before the Gentiles and their kings and before the people of Israel. ¹⁶I will show him how much he must suffer for my name."

Acts 18:9-10 ❦ ⁹"Do not be afraid; keep on speaking, do not be silent. ¹⁰For I am with you, and no one is going to attack and harm you, because I have many people in this city."

See also *Mark 9:50; John 16:33; Acts 22:7-8,10,18,21; 23:11; 26:14-18.*

PEACE

John 14:27 27"Peace I leave with you; my peace I give you. I do not give to you as the world gives. Do not let your hearts be troubled and do not be afraid."

PERSECUTION

Matthew 10:17-23 17"Be on your guard against men; they will hand you over to the local councils and flog you in their synagogues. 18On my account you will be brought before governors and kings as witnesses to them and to the Gentiles. 19But when they arrest you, do not worry about what to say or how to say it. At that time you will be given what to say, 20for it will not be you speaking, but the Spirit of your Father speaking through you. 21Brother will betray brother to death, and a father his child; children will rebel against their parents and have them put to death. [22]All men will hate you because of me, but he who stands firm to the end will be saved. [23]When you are persecuted in one place, flee to another. I tell you the truth, you will not finish going through the cities of Israel before the Son of Man comes."

See also *Matthew 10:24-39.*

PRAYER

Matthew 6:5-13 [5]"And when you pray, do not be like the hypocrites, for they love to pray standing in the synagogues and on the street corners to be seen by men. I tell you the truth, they have received their reward in full. [6]But when you pray, go into your room, close the door and pray to your Father, who is unseen. Then your Father, who sees what is done in secret, will reward you. [7]And when you pray, do not keep on babbling like pagans, for they think they will be heard because of their many words. [8]Do not be like them, for your Father knows what you need before you ask him. [9]This, then, is how you should pray: 'Our Father in heaven, hallowed be your name, [10]your kingdom come, your will be done on earth as it is in heaven. ¹¹Give us today our daily bread. ¹²Forgive us our debts, as we also have forgiven our debtors. ¹³And lead us not into temptation, but deliver us from the evil one.'"

Matthew 7:7-11 ⁷"Ask and it will be given to you; seek and you will find; knock and the door will be opened to you. ⁸For everyone who asks receives; he who seeks finds; and to him who knocks, the door will be opened. ⁹Which of you, if his son asks for bread, will give him a stone? ¹⁰Or if he asks for a fish, will give him a snake? ¹¹If you, then, though you are evil, know how to give good gifts to your children, how much more will your Father in heaven give good gifts to those who ask him!"

See also *Matthew 18:18-20; 21:13,21-22; Mark 11:17; Luke 11:2-13; 19:46; John 14:12-14; 16:23-24.*

REJECTION

Mark 6:4 ⁴"Only in his hometown, among his relatives and in his own house is a prophet without honor."

See also *Matthew 13:57.*

REPENTANCE

Matthew 4:17 ❧ ¹⁷"Repent, for the kingdom of heaven is near."

Luke 13:2-5 ❧ ²"Do you think that these Galileans were worse sinners than all the other Galileans because they suffered this way? ³I tell you, no! But unless you repent, you too will all perish. ⁴Or those eighteen who died when the tower in Siloam fell on them—do you think they were more guilty than all the others living in Jerusalem? ⁵I tell you, no! But unless you repent, you too will all perish."

See also *Mark 1:15.*

REST

Matthew 11:27-30 ❧ ²⁷"All things have been committed to me by my Father. No one knows the Son except the Father, and no one knows the Father except the Son and those to whom the Son chooses to reveal him. ²⁸Come to me, all you who are weary and burdened, and I will give you rest. ²⁹Take my yoke upon you and learn from me, for I am gentle and humble in heart, and you will find rest for your souls. ³⁰For my yoke is easy and my burden is light."

See also *Mark 6:31.*

RESURRECTION

Matthew 22:29-32 ⟶ ²⁹"You are in error because you do not know the Scriptures or the power of God. ³⁰At the resurrection people will neither marry nor be given in marriage; they will be like the angels in heaven. ³¹But about the resurrection of the dead—have you not read what God said to you, ³²'I am the God of Abraham, the God of Isaac, and the God of Jacob'? He is not the God of the dead but of the living."

John 11:25-26 ⟶ ²⁵"I am the resurrection and the life. He who believes in me will live, even though he dies; ²⁶and whoever lives and believes in me will never die. Do you believe this?"

See also *Luke 24:17,19,25-26,36-39,41,44,46-49.*

REVERENCE

Matthew 10:26-28,32-33 ⟶ ²⁶"So do not be afraid of them. There is nothing concealed that will not be disclosed, or hidden that will not be made known. ²⁷What I tell you in the dark, speak in the daylight; what is whispered in your ear, proclaim from the roofs. ²⁸Do not be afraid of those who kill the body but cannot kill the soul. Rather, be afraid of the One who can destroy both soul and body in hell...³²Whoever acknowledges me before men, I will also acknowledge him before my Father in heaven. ³³But whoever disowns me before men, I will disown him before my Father in heaven."

Luke 12:4-5,8-10 ⁴"I tell you, my friends, do not be afraid of those who kill the body and after that can do no more. ⁵But I will show you whom you should fear: Fear him who, after the killing of the body, has power to throw you into hell. Yes, I tell you, fear him...⁸I tell you, whoever acknowledges me before men, the Son of Man will also acknowledge him before the angels of God. ⁹But he who disowns me before men will be disowned before the angels of God. ¹⁰And everyone who speaks a word against the Son of Man will be forgiven, but anyone who blasphemes against the Holy Spirit will not be forgiven."

RIGHTEOUS LIVING

Matthew 5:33-42 ⟨≈⟩ ³³"Again, you have heard that it was said to the people long ago, 'Do not break your oath, but keep the oaths you have made to the Lord.' ³⁴But I tell you, Do not swear at all: either by heaven, for it is God's throne; ³⁵or by the earth, for it is his footstool; or by Jerusalem, for it is the city of the Great King. ³⁶And do not swear by your head, for you cannot make even one hair white or black. ³⁷Simply let your 'Yes' be 'Yes,' and your 'No,' 'No'; anything beyond this comes from the evil one. ³⁸You have heard that it was said, 'Eye for eye, and tooth for tooth.' ³⁹But I tell you, Do not resist an evil person. If someone strikes you on the right cheek, turn to him the other also. ⁴⁰And if someone wants to sue you and take your tunic, let him have your cloak as well. ⁴¹If someone forces you to go one mile, go with him two miles. ⁴²Give to the one who asks you, and do not turn away from the one who wants to borrow from you."

Matthew 6:1-4 ⟨≈⟩ ¹"Be careful not to do your 'acts of righteousness' before men, to be seen by them. If you do, you will have no reward from your Father in heaven. ²So when you give to the needy, do not announce it with trumpets, as the hypocrites do in the synagogues and on the streets, to be honored by men. I tell you the truth, they have received their reward in full. ³But when you give to the needy, do not let your left hand know what your right hand is doing, ⁴so that your giving may be in secret. Then your Father, who sees what is done in secret, will reward you."

Matthew 7:13-14 ⤜ ¹³"Enter through the narrow gate. For wide is the gate and broad is the road that leads to destruction, and many enter through it. ¹⁴But small is the gate and narrow the road that leads to life, and only a few find it."

SABBATH

Matthew 12:3-8,11-12 ⤜ ³"Haven't you read what David did when he and his companions were hungry? ⁴He entered the house of God, and he and his companions ate the consecrated bread—which was not lawful for them to do, but only for the priests. ⁵Or haven't you read in the Law that on the Sabbath the priests in the temple desecrate the day and yet are innocent? ⁶I tell you that one greater than the temple is here. ⁷If you had known what these words mean, 'I desire mercy, not sacrifice,' you would not have condemned the innocent. ⁸For the Son of Man is Lord of the Sabbath...¹¹If any of you has a sheep and it falls into a pit on the Sabbath, will you not take hold of it and lift it out? ¹²How much more valuable is a man than a sheep! Therefore it is lawful to do good on the Sabbath."

John 7:21-24 ²¹"I did one miracle, and you are all astonished. ²²Yet because Moses gave you circumcision (though actually it did not come from Moses, but from the patriarchs), you circumcise a child on the Sabbath. ²³Now if a child can be circumcised on the Sabbath so that the law of Moses may not be broken, why are you angry with me for healing the whole man on the Sabbath? ²⁴Stop judging by mere appearances, and make a right judgment."

See also *Matthew 12:13; 24:20; Mark 2:25-28; Luke 6:3-5,8-10; 13:15-16; 14:3,5.*

SALVATION

Matthew 9:12-13 ❧ [12]"It is not the healthy who need a doctor, but the sick. [13]But go and learn what this means: 'I desire mercy, not sacrifice.' For I have not come to call the righteous, but sinners."

Mark 10:45 ❧ [45]"For even the Son of Man did not come to be served, but to serve, and to give his life as a ransom for many."

See also *Matthew 8:14; Mark 2:17; Luke 5:31-32; 19:10; John 14:6; Revelation 3:20.*

SATAN

Matthew 12:25-28 ❧ [25]"Every kingdom divided against itself will be ruined, and every city or household divided against itself will not stand. [26]If Satan drives out Satan, he is divided against himself. How then can his kingdom stand? [27]And if I drive out demons by Beelzebub, by whom do your people drive them out? So then, they will be your judges. [28]But if I drive out demons by the Spirit of God, then the kingdom of God has come upon you."

Matthew 16:23 ⬥ ²³"Get behind me, Satan! You are a stumbling block to me; you do not have in mind the things of God, but the things of men."

Luke 10:18-20 ⬥ ¹⁸"I saw Satan fall like lightning from heaven. ¹⁹I have given you authority to trample on snakes and scorpions and to overcome all the power of the enemy; nothing will harm you. ²⁰However, do not rejoice that the spirits submit to you, but rejoice that your names are written in heaven."

See also *Matthew 12:29-30; Mark 3:23-27; 8:33.*

SERVANTHOOD

Matthew 10:40-42 ⬥ ⁴⁰"He who receives you receives me, and he who receives me receives the one who sent me. ⁴¹Anyone who receives a prophet because he is a prophet will receive a prophet's reward, and anyone who receives a righteous man because he is a righteous man will receive a righteous man's reward. ⁴²And if anyone gives even a cup of cold water to one of these little ones because he is my disciple, I tell you the truth, he will certainly not lose his reward."

Matthew 20:25-28 ²⁵"You know that the rulers of the Gentiles lord it over them, and their high officials exercise authority over them. ²⁶Not so with you. Instead, whoever wants to become great among you must be your servant, ²⁷and whoever wants to be first must be your slave—²⁸just as the Son of Man did not come to be served, but to serve, and to give his life as a ransom for many."

See also *Matthew 6:24; Mark 9:33-35; 10:36,38-40,42-45; Luke 16:13; 17:7-10; 22:25-30; John 13:7-8,10-17.*

SHEEP AND GOATS

Matthew 25:31-40 ³¹"When the Son of Man comes in his glory, and all the angels with him, he will sit on his throne in heavenly glory. ³²All the nations will be gathered before him, and he will separate the people one from another as a shepherd separates the sheep from the goats. ³³He will put the sheep on his right and the goats on his left. ³⁴Then the King will say to those on his right, 'Come, you who are blessed by my Father;

take your inheritance, the kingdom prepared for you since the creation of the world. ³⁵For I was hungry and you gave me something to eat, I was thirsty and you gave me something to drink, I was a stranger and you invited me in, ³⁶I needed clothes and you clothed me, I was sick and you looked after me, I was in prison and you came to visit me.' ³⁷Then the righteous will answer him, 'Lord, when did we see you hungry and feed you, or thirsty and give you something to drink? ³⁸When did we see you a stranger and invite you in, or needing clothes and clothe you? ³⁹When did we see you sick or in prison and go to visit you?' ⁴⁰The King will reply, 'I tell you the truth, whatever you did for one of the least of these brothers of mine, you did for me.'"

See also *Matthew 25:41-46.*

SIGNS

Matthew 12:39-42 ³⁹"A wicked and adulterous generation asks for a miraculous sign! But none will be given it except the sign of the prophet Jonah. ⁴⁰For as Jonah was three days and three nights in the belly of a huge fish, so the Son of Man will be three days and three nights in the heart of the earth. ⁴¹The men of Nineveh will stand up at the judgment with this generation and condemn it; for they repented at the preaching of Jonah, and now one greater than Jonah is here. ⁴²The Queen of the South will rise at the judgment with this generation and condemn it; for she came from the ends of the earth to listen to Solomon's wisdom, and now one greater than Solomon is here."

Matthew 16:2-4 ✎ ²"When evening comes, you say, 'It will be fair weather, for the sky is red,' ³and in the morning, 'Today it will be stormy, for the sky is red and overcast.' You know how to interpret the appearance of the sky, but you cannot interpret the signs of the times. ⁴A wicked and adulterous generation looks for a miraculous sign, but none will be given it except the sign of Jonah."

Mark 8:12 ✎ ¹²"Why does this generation ask for a miraculous sign? I tell you the truth, no sign will be given to it."

See also *Luke 11:29-32*.

SIN

Matthew 5:19-20 ⟶ ¹⁹"Anyone who breaks one of the least of these commandments and teaches others to do the same will be called least in the kingdom of heaven, but whoever practices and teaches these commands will be called great in the kingdom of heaven. ²⁰For I tell you that unless your righteousness surpasses that of the Pharisees and the teachers of the law, you will certainly not enter the kingdom of heaven."

Matthew 18:8-9 ⟶ ⁸"If your hand or your foot causes you to sin cut it off and throw it away. It is better for you to enter life maimed or crippled than to have two hands or two feet and be thrown into eternal fire. ⁹And if your eye causes you to sin, gouge it out and throw it away. It is better for you to enter life with one eye than to have two eyes and be thrown into the fire of hell."

Matthew 18:15-17 ⟶ ¹⁵"If your brother sins against you, go and show him his fault, just between the two of you. If he listens to you, you have won your brother over. ¹⁶But if he will not listen, take one or two others along, so that 'every matter may be established by the testimony of two or three witnesses.' ¹⁷If he refuses to listen to them, tell it to the church; and if he refuses to listen even to the church, treat him as you would a pagan or a tax collector."

SOVEREIGNTY OF GOD

Revelation 1:8,17-18 ⟋ ⁸"I am the Alpha and the Omega, who is, and who was, and who is to come, the Almighty...¹⁷Do not be afraid. I am the First and the Last. ¹⁸I am the Living One; I was dead, and behold I am alive for ever and ever! And I hold the keys of death and Hades."

SPEECH

Matthew 12:36-37 ⟋ ³⁶"But I tell you that men will have to give account on the day of judgment for every careless word they have spoken. ³⁷For by your words you will be acquitted, and by your words you will be condemned."

TAXES

Matthew 17:25-27 ⟋ ²⁵"What do you think, Simon?...From whom do the kings of the earth collect duty and taxes—from their own sons or from others? ²⁶[If they collect duty and taxes from others, then] the sons are exempt...²⁷But so that we may not offend them, go to the lake and throw out your line. Take the first fish you catch; open its mouth and you will find a four-drachma coin. Take it and give it to them for my tax and yours."

Matthew 22:18-21 ⭒ ¹⁸"You hypocrites, why are you trying to trap me? ¹⁹Show me the coin used for paying the tax. ²⁰Whose portrait is this? And whose inscription? ²¹Give to Caesar what is Caesar's, and to God what is God's."

See also *Mark 12:15-17; Luke 20:24-25.*

TEMPLE

Matthew 21:13 ⭒ ¹³"It it written...'My house will be called a house of prayer,' but you are making it a 'den of robbers.'"

Luke 2:49 ⭒ ⁴⁹"Why were you searching for me?...Didn't you know I had to be in my Father's house?"

See also *Mark 11:17; John 2:16,19.*

TEMPTATION

Matthew 26:41 ᘓ᙮ᘐ ⁴¹"Watch and pray so that you will not fall into temptation. The spirit is willing, but the body is weak."

Mark 9:43,45,47-50 ᘓ᙮ᘐ ⁴³"If your hand causes you to sin, cut it off. It is better for you to enter life maimed than with two hands to go into hell, where the fire never goes out…⁴⁵And if your foot causes you to sin, cut it off. It is better for you to enter life crippled than to have two feet and be thrown into hell…⁴⁷And if your eye causes you to sin, pluck it out. It is better for you to enter the kingdom of God with one eye than to have two eyes and be thrown into hell, ⁴⁸where 'their worm does not die, and the fire is not quenched.' ⁴⁹Everyone will be salted with fire. ⁵⁰Salt is good, but if it loses its saltiness, how can you make it salty again? Have salt in yourselves, and be at peace with each other."

See also *Matthew 4:1-11; 18:7-9; Luke 17:1-2; 22:40,46.*

TRANSFIGURATION

Matthew 17:7,9,11-12 ᘓ᙮ᘐ ⁷ [To his disciples] "Get

up…Don't be afraid…⁹Don't tell anyone what you have seen, until the Son of Man has been raised from the dead…¹¹To be sure, Elijah comes and will restore all things. ¹²But I tell you, Elijah has already come, and they did not recognize him, but have done to him everything they wished. In the same way the Son of Man is going to suffer at their hands."

TREASURE IN HEAVEN

Matthew 6:19-21 ⬥ ¹⁹"Do not store up for yourselves treasures on earth, where moth and rust destroy, and where thieves break in and steal. ²⁰But store up for yourselves treasures in heaven, where moth and rust do not destroy, and where thieves do not break in and steal. ²¹For where your treasure is, there your heart will be also."

Matthew 19:21 ⬥ ²¹"If you want to be perfect, go, sell your possessions and give to the poor, and you will have treasure in heaven. Then come, follow me."

See also *Luke 12:15-21,33-34; 18:22.*

TRUTH AND FREEDOM

John 8:31-32,34-36 ◇◇◇ ³¹"If you hold to my teaching, you are really my disciples. ³²Then you will know the truth, and the truth will set you free...³⁴I tell you the truth, everyone who sins is a slave to sin. ³⁵Now a slave has no permanent place in the family, but a son belongs to it forever. ³⁶So if the Son sets you free, you will be free indeed."

UNPARDONABLE SIN

Matthew 12:30-32 ◇◇◇ ³⁰"He who is not with me is against me, and he who does not gather with me scatters. ³¹And so I tell you, every sin and blasphemy will be forgiven man, but the blasphemy against the Spirit will not be forgiven. ³²Anyone who speaks a word against the Son of Man will be forgiven, but anyone who speaks against the Holy Spirit will not be forgiven, either in this age or in the age to come."

See also *Mark 3:28-29; Luke 12:10.*

WATCHFULNESS

Matthew 24:42-51 ◇◇◇ ⁴²"Therefore keep watch, because you do not know on what day your Lord will come. ⁴³But understand this: If the owner of the house had known at what time of night the thief was coming, he would have kept watch and would not have let his house be broken into. ⁴⁴So you also must be ready, because the Son of Man will come at an hour when you do not expect him. ⁴⁵Who then is the faithful and wise servant, whom the master has put in charge of the servants in his household to give them their food at the proper time? ⁴⁶It will be good for that servant whose master finds him doing so when he returns. ⁴⁷I tell you the truth, he will put him in charge of all his possessions. ⁴⁸But suppose that servant is wicked and says to himself, 'My master is staying away a long time,' ⁴⁹and he then begins to beat his fellow servants and to eat and drink with drunkards. ⁵⁰The master of that servant will come on a day when he does not expect him and at an hour he is not aware of. ⁵¹He will cut him to pieces and assign him a place with the hypocrites, where there will be weeping and gnashing of teeth."

See also *Mark 13:32-37; Luke 12:35-40; 21:34-36.*

WILL OF GOD

Mark 3:33-35 ⟱ ³³"Who are my mother and my brothers? ³⁴[The people who are sitting around me] are my mother and brothers! ³⁵Whoever does God's will is my brother and sister and mother."

John 4:32,34 ⟱ ³²"I have food to eat that you know nothing about...³⁴My food...is to do the will of him who sent me and to finish his work."

WINE INTO NEW WINESKINS

Matthew 9:16-17 ⟱ ¹⁶"No one sews a patch of unshrunk cloth on an old garment, for the patch will pull away from the garment, making the tear worse. ¹⁷Neither do men pour new wine into old wineskins. If they do, the skins will burst, the wine will run out and the wineskins will be ruined. No, they pour new wine into new wineskins, and both are preserved."

See also *Mark 2:21-22; Luke 5:36-39*.

WOES

Luke 10:13-15 ⟱ ¹³"Woe to you, Korazin! Woe to you, Bethsaida! For if the miracles that were performed in you had been performed in Tyre and Sidon, they would have repented long ago, sitting in sackcloth and ashes. [14]But it will be more bearable for Tyre and Sidon at the judgment than for you. [15]And you, Capernaum, will you be lifted up to the skies? No, you will go down to the depths."

Luke 11:39-44,46-52 [39]"Now then, you Pharisees clean the outside of the cup and dish, but inside you are full of greed and wickedness. [40]You foolish people! Did not the one who made the outside make the inside also? [41]But give what is inside...to the poor, and everything will be clean for you. [42]Woe to you Pharisees, because you give God a tenth of your mint, rue and all other kinds of garden herbs, but you neglect justice and the love of God. You should have practiced the latter without leaving the former undone. [43]Woe to you Pharisees, because you love the most important seats in the synagogues and greetings in the marketplaces. [44]Woe to you, because you are like unmarked graves, which men walk over without knowing it...[46]And you experts in the law, woe to you, because you load people down with burdens they can hardly carry, and you yourselves will not lift one finger to help them. [47]Woe to you, because you build tombs for the prophets, and it was your forefathers who killed them. [48]So you testify that you approve of what your forefathers did; they killed the prophets, and you build their tombs. [49]Because of this, God in his wisdom said, 'I will send them prophets and apostles, some of whom they will kill and others they will persecute.' [50]Therefore this generation will be held responsible for the blood of all the prophets that has been shed since the beginning of the world, [51]from the blood of Abel to the blood of Zechariah, who was killed between the altar and the sanctuary. Yes, I tell you, this generation will be held responsible for it all. [52]Woe to you experts in the law, because you have taken away the key to knowledge. You yourselves have not entered, and you have hindered those who were entering."

See also *Matthew 23:2-36; Luke 6:24-26; 10:16.*

WOMAN AT THE WELL

John 4:7,10,13-14,16-18,21-24,26 ∽∽ [7]"Will

you give me a drink?…[10]If you knew the gift of God and who it is that asks you for a drink, you would have asked him and he would have given you living water…[13]Everyone who drinks this water [from the well] will be thirsty again, [14]but whoever drinks the water I give him will never thirst. Indeed, the water I give him will become in him a spring of water welling up to eternal life…[16]Go, call your husband and come back. [17]You are right when you say you have no husband. [18]The fact is, you have had five husbands, and the man you now have is not your husband. What you have just said is quite true…[21]Believe me, woman, a time is coming when you will worship the Father neither on this mountain nor in Jerusalem. [22]You Samaritans worship what you do not know; we worship what we do know, for salvation is from the Jews. [23]Yet a time is coming and has now come when the true worshipers will worship the Father in spirit and truth, for they are the kind of worshipers the Father seeks. [24]God is spirit, and his worshipers must worship in spirit and in truth…[26]I who speak to you am he [the Messiah]."

WOMAN IN ADULTERY

John 8:7,10-11 ◦◦◦ ⁷"If any one of you [teachers of the law and Pharisees] is without sin, let him be the first to throw a stone at her...¹⁰Woman, where are they? Has no one condemned you? ¹¹Then neither do I condemn you...Go now and leave your life of sin."

WORLD (HATES JESUS)

John 7:6-8 ◦◦◦ ⁶"The right time for me has not yet come; for you any time is right. ⁷The world cannot hate you, but it hates me because I testify that what it does is evil. ⁸You go to the Feast. I am not yet going up to this Feast, because for me the right time has not yet come."

John 15:18-25 ◦◦◦ ¹⁸"If the world hates you, keep in mind that it hated me first. ¹⁹If you belonged to the world, it would love you as its own. As it is, you do not belong to the world, but I have chosen you out of the world. That is why the world hates you. ²⁰Remember the words I spoke to you: 'No servant is greater than his master.' If they persecuted me, they will persecute you also. If they obeyed my teaching, they will obey yours also. ²¹They will treat you this way because of my name, for they do not know the One who sent me. ²²If I had not come and spoken to them, they would not be guilty of sin. Now, however, they have no excuse for their sin. ²³He who hates me hates my Father as well. ²⁴If I had not done among them what no one else did, they would not be guilty of sin. But now they have seen these miracles, and yet they have hated both me and my Father. ²⁵But this is to fulfill what is written in their Law: 'They hated me without reason.'"

WORRY

Matthew 6:25-27,34 ²⁵"Therefore I tell you, do not worry about your life, what you will eat or drink; or about your body, what you will wear. Is not life more important than food, and the body more important than clothes? ²⁶Look at the birds of the air; they do not sow or reap or store away in barns, and yet your heavenly Father feeds them. Are you not much more valuable than they? ²⁷Who of you by worrying can add a single hour to his life?…³⁴Therefore do not worry about tomorrow, for tomorrow will worry about itself. Each day has enough trouble of its own."

See also *Matthew 6:28-33; 10:28-31; Luke 12:6-7,22-31.*

WORSHIP

Matthew 4:10 ¹⁰"Away from me, Satan! For it is written: 'Worship the Lord your God, and serve him only.'"

Matthew 21:16 ¹⁶"Yes, [I hear what these children who are singing 'Hosana' to me are saying]...have you never read, 'From the lips of children and infants you have ordained praise'?"

Mark 14:6-9 ⁶"Leave her alone...Why are you bothering her? She has done a beautiful thing to me. ⁷The poor you will always have with you, and you can help them any time you want. But you will not always have me. ⁸She did what she could. She poured perfume on my body beforehand to prepare for my burial. ⁹I tell you the truth, wherever the gospel is preached throughout the world, what she has done will also be told, in memory of her."

See also *Luke 19:40; John 4:21-24; 12:7-8.*